THIRTY-TWO ORDINARY WOMEN WITH EXTRAORDINARY STORIES

Women *of a* Certain Age

ANSWER SEVEN QUESTIONS

About Life, Love, and Loss

Joan Kennedy

INDIE BOOKS
INTERNATIONAL

ISBN-10: 1-941870-76-7
ISBN-13: 978-1-941870-76-1
Library of Congress Control Number: 2016959731

Designed by Joni McPherson, mcphersongraphics.com

INDIE BOOKS INTERNATIONAL, LLC
2424 VISTA WAY, SUITE 316
OCEANSIDE, CA 92054
www.indiebooksintl.com

For quantity pricing, please contact publisher
or the co-author you purchased your book from.

Dedication

*To those women who opened their minds and
generously shared their stories of courage, passion,
adventure and misfortune. Their lives made
"Women of a Certain Age," possible.*

*It is my sincere hope this series will touch
the hearts of many and inspire others to believe in
themselves, take action and dream a bigger dream.*

Joan

Foreword

In the 70s, Joan Kennedy was in her fashion career when she was asked to give a presentation to a classroom of students. Her presentation was fine and when hands were raised and excuses were given to her, she loudly proclaimed, "Set some goals!" That day she encouraged them to decide what they wanted in their careers and lives. She was asked to come back, only this time to speak on goal-setting, not fashion. Little did she know that her life would never be the same.

She went on to publish her first book, *I Don't Want Much Out of Life, I Want More.* Joan has been writing and speaking nationally for over forty years.

In 1982, at twenty-one, I met Joan Kennedy. Little did I know my life would never be the same. Joan invited me to attend the Minnesota Chapter of the National Speakers Association. Later that year, Joan introduced me to Og Mandino, one of my heroes and the author of *The Greatest Salesman in the World.*

Over the years, Joan and I spent a good deal of time together. Joan is a remarkable force for good in the world. Her well of wisdom, stories that touch the heart, and ideas worth sharing will stand the test of time. Now, at the young age of ninety-four, Joan is still inspiring others, dispelling the myths of aging, and writing her next book. When asked about retirement, she whispers, "I still have my work to do."

Women of a Certain Age will engage your mind and stir your soul. The stories of these courageous women will remind you to examine your life and work. It may trigger an idea or reconnect you to a dream delayed. Hopefully, you will never be the same after reading these incredible stories.

Please consider sharing Joan's book with others. It is the perfect gift for your mother, a sister, daughter, niece, granddaughter, friend, or colleague. Together, let's share the good news that anything is possible and that who you are matters.

Mark LeBlanc
Speaker, pilgrim, and author of *Never Be the Same* and *Growing Your Business!*

Preface

Life is either a grand adventure, or it's nothing!
HELEN KELLER

I am delighted to bring to light the personal stories of thirty-two women of a certain age.

To find women who had a story to tell, and would want to share their stories in this book, was quite a journey. It lasted more than a year. I had several women who wanted to write their story, but decided not to because they found it too difficult.

As the women started sending in their stories, I found them to be not only interesting, but varied, and some, surprising. They told about their encounters with loss, difficult times, and unimaginable experiences.

The qualities that helped these women to surmount their difficulties were perseverance, persistence, the ability to start over again, and making necessary changes that life called for.

I feel honored by the willingness of the women in this book who told their stories of what life demanded of them, and went beyond their self-doubts and fears.

From these inspiring stories you may realize no matter the difficult life experiences, there is always hope for the future.

Joan Kennedy

Acknowledgments

I would like to extend my deeply felt thanks to Gloria VanDemmeltraadt, who skillfully edited this book, making suggestions and sharing ideas. She was easy to work with, always upbeat, patient, and positive. She was focused and deeply involved in the book, and supported me all the way in making this book a reality.

I want to thank Louise Griffith, who helped find interesting women with equally interesting stories.

And finally, I would like to thank all the women, who were open to sharing their incredible stories of the ups and downs of their lives well lived.

This quote from Tina Turner expresses my gratitude to all of them: "I learned something from every step in my life, and I became strong."

The Questions

Each contributing author was asked the following questions around which to build her story:

1. What experiences prepared you for this period in your life?

2. What was the biggest challenge you overcame?

3. Have your wants and desires changed over the last ten years?

4. What are your future plans?

5. What are you happy with right now?

6. How do you have fun?

7. Knowing what you know now, if you could go back to give yourself a piece of advice when you turned eighteen, what would you tell yourself?

Table of Contents

In Our Twenties

In Our Thirties

In Our Forties

In Our Fifties

In Our Sixties

In Our Seventies

In Our Eighties

In Our Nineties

In Our Twenties

Early Midlife Crisis
Nikki Abramson

Common knowledge is that we can anticipate a midlife crisis in our forties. I believe many people can also go through such a crisis in their twenties as well. You graduate from college and then boom—you are no longer living in a dorm. Instead, you are on your own, paying your bills and loans, and striving to figure out what you will actually do with your degree. In my case, I graduated and moved home to live with my parents, something many of my colleagues were doing at the time. I graduated in the great recession when no one was getting jobs.

Like many of my friends, I experienced this type of twenties crisis, but I had a second crisis that not as many twenty-somethings go through. I had a health crisis. Let me back up for a moment to one of the biggest challenges I have had to overcome.

In 2009, I graduated with a Bachelor of Arts degree in elementary education from Bethel University, in St. Paul, Minnesota. I was a naive, excited, young woman ready to take on the world. My image of the future changed in August, 2010, when I was in a car accident. My car was totaled—the car I had gotten for my sixteenth birthday. At first I thought

I only had a minor headache and whiplash. A week later, my body was flung into full body muscle spasms that left me bedridden for seven months. It took several months for me to learn I was experiencing a devastating condition called dystonia. I lost my hope and dreams of teaching. I couldn't drive or work full-time. I was not only dealing with a medical condition that is still causing painful involuntary muscle spasms, but also one that drastically changed the course of my life.

The strength to deal with this new reality stems from growing up with other medical challenges and from being an adopted person of color. Having gone through adversity in the past, I already had the tools to overcome even the most challenging times ahead. My health challenges forced me to develop new skills and pushed me into a new career: motivational coaching and speaking.

Now that I am nearing thirty years old, I realize I have many things to be grateful for. I am happy with the relationships I have made since my accident and with my new career path. I appreciate the support I have received from family and friends. Happiness comes from being grateful for what I have, rather than focusing on what I don't have.

During my crisis, I thought about what I didn't have: I didn't have a career; I wasn't making much money; I wasn't able to drive; I wasn't able to keep up with my peers. Now I realize that happiness comes from deep within. I now view my twenties, in spite of the challenges, as being some of the best years.

For me, having fun comes with daily life. I love life. Because of this, every day I have fun. Because of my medical challenges, having fun is simply spending time with others and it's an added bonus if food is involved. Going to Chanhassen Dinner Theatre, Guthrie Theater, and The Orpheum Theatre in Minneapolis are truly some of my favorite places to go during my "fun" time, especially doing it with people I love. I love theatre, and especially musical theatre. I also love playing board games and spending time in the sun. Traveling is a huge part of my life where I can also have fun. Because at this point in my life I am not tied down to anything (a relationship, a job, family, etc.), I have the flexibility and freedom to travel and visit friends in various parts of the country.

I was a senior in high school when I turned eighteen years old. As an eighteen-year-old, my focus and energy was spent on schoolwork, friends, and college. My eighteen-year-old self was scared, nervous, and worried about the future. I wanted to do well in school. I wanted to find a college that was a good fit for me. I worried about staying close to my high-school friends. I was filled with the "what ifs" in life.

If I could go back in time and give my eighteen-year-old self a piece of advice, I would tell myself to let go. There is a plan for you. Trust in the plan and go with the flow. It will work out. I would tell the eighteen-year-old Nikki to be in the moment, enjoy life, and be grateful for what you have. Each year presents itself with its own challenges, and we don't know what they will be. I would tell myself that wherever you go to school, whatever your ACT score was, whatever you major in, will not define you. It is our character and the person we become that is important. Finally, I would give myself the advice to create time and space for myself. During my school years, I tried to be the perfect student. I would tell myself to slow down and do things that were important to me.

Ten years ago, on graduating from high school and entering college, my wants and desires were to meet new friends, retain my high-school friends/teachers, and start a new chapter in life, focusing on a teaching career. My wants and desires were selfish. Now, my wants and desires are much more people-first. My goal is to change the world, one person at a time. I want to make an impact on the world through my teaching, speaking, and performances. I want to deepen relationships with family and friends and hopefully find "Mr. Right." I would love to become financially stable and have an effective health support system. Whether those things occur or not, I want to continue giving myself time and grace when, due to health issues, I run into my limits. I look forward to what the future may hold, but I will also live in the moment with an attitude of gratitude.

Embracing Uncertainty
Anna Bosak

So far, my twenties have felt rather unsettled and challenging. I think two major experiences have prepared me to handle the ups and downs of this period in my life—my time at Grinnell College, and moving to Spain to teach English for a year following college. Both of those experiences stem from decisions in which I chose to try the unexpected and unknown. I trace a lot of changes in myself back to Grinnell College. I was thrown into a very intensive, immersive experience with a tremendously diverse group of intelligent and talented people, and I was constantly pushed and challenged. I honestly can't imagine who I would be if I hadn't gone to Grinnell.

After college, I made what felt was a bit of a rash decision to move to Spain and teach English in a public school. In retrospect, it was the perfect thing for me to do. I jumped into something I wasn't at all prepared for and came out the other side with incredible memories and a new level of confidence.

I have a sense that I haven't even come close to yet experiencing a major challenge in my life. Not to say there haven't been difficult periods, or tough decisions, but I'm fortunate enough to say nothing I've had to face so far has really kept me down for long. I had a happy childhood, went off to a great college, got to travel internationally, and landed in a career I enjoy. I've always hated questions about the biggest challenge I've faced, since I end up comparing my seemingly small challenges with much more dramatic events others have faced. I feel like I might be tempting fate to say I haven't had a major challenge, but I try to keep the perspective in mind that you never know what will come, and when a setback does happen, I'll just try to approach it calmly and bravely.

What I want for my life is still constantly changing, but I think how I decide what I want at this moment is a much more individual and independent process than it was ten years ago. When I was younger, I don't think I had enough perspective or variety of experiences to honestly think through what made sense for me, and I thought about what I wanted for my future as having to fit into some normal or standard progression or set of options. Now, I feel incredibly less constrained by external pressures when thinking about what I want, and I'm letting myself continue to explore and change my ideas about what I want.

For good or bad, I've grown out of the habit I used to have of looking far ahead into my future and attempting to plan out every detail. This doesn't mean I don't have some vision of what I'd like my future to look like. In the next five years, I'm considering getting an MBA, I'd like to move toward buying a home, and hopefully I'll be married, or headed that way and thinking about having children. I'm not letting those long-term plans keep me from being open to new and unexpected opportunities, though. Right now,

I'm more likely to enjoy planning out my next big trip than picturing exactly what my days will look like in ten years. I haven't stuck to any of the plans I had for myself when I was in high school, and I'm glad! I think my plans for myself tended to be based on expectations or perceptions of where I should be headed, and as I move toward making plans based on what I really need and want, my plans have much more flexibility.

Right now, I'm happy with how I'm spending my days. For the first time in a while, I feel fairly settled, and like I'm beginning to put down roots. I'm in a job where I can see myself staying for more than a year or two; I'm building a solid community of friends in my community while trying to stay connected to friends living far away; I'm very close with my family; and I'm actually starting to feel empowered in being able to shape my life for myself. I'm not sure I am where I expected I would be at twenty-five, but I enjoy the pattern of my days and I'm hopeful for what the future will bring.

In the last few years, I've started to make fun a higher priority. I have a tendency to be very goal-oriented and driven, which can be great, but can make it hard to step back and just relax. I'm making more time in my life for music (playing piano and singing with friends), exploring my neighborhood (taking advantage of the culturally diverse area I live in, and always trying new restaurants), travel, cooking, and reading, which I have always loved. I've also found that self-care can be very enjoyable—I'm much calmer and happier when I'm exercising, practicing yoga, going to church, and just taking time to have a quiet moment alone—all things I used to view as a chore rather than fun. Most importantly, I'm trying to stop thinking about how something I enjoy doing will appear to other people, and just focusing on pursuing whatever I find to be genuinely fun.

My eighteen-year-old self is starting to feel very distant. I've grown and changed so much in only seven years. If I could tell that version of me anything, it would be to worry less, put less pressure on myself, and to be more open to the unknown and unexpected. When I think about the most rewarding or formative experiences I've had since I was eighteen, they haven't come from measuring up to anyone else's expectations for myself or doing exactly what everyone else was doing. Instead, they came from taking risks, being brave, having confidence in myself, and embracing uncertainty. I plan to take this approach, which I did not when I was eighteen, with me through the rest of my twenties and beyond.

Living the Dream
Hannah Neuman

I don't feel that anyone is ever "prepared" for what life throws at you; you simply live and learn, sometimes a hundred times over and over. In my twenty-two years of life, I feel I have been through more than most. I have made mistake after mistake and made some bad choices. Plus, some things I didn't have the option of making a choice about, whether it be losing my dad, to being in an abusive relationship, to dealing with personal medical issues. With the strength of my mom and the relationships I have since built, I have learned these situations and circumstances have shaped me to be the person I am each day. I choose not to dwell on the negative and to thrive on the positive.

When I was two years old, my mom and dad got divorced. My mom remarried just two years later to a man I would look to as my "real dad" for the next seventeen years of my life. Throughout my childhood and into my teen years, my dad was very sick. Most holidays and birthdays were spent in and out of the hospital. It seemed to become our second home. In 2012, my dad gained his wings. At nineteen years old, I struggled to understand why. Why did he have to go? Why was his life taken so soon? I grappled for the next two years wondering what I had done to deserve to lose him and why my biological father wanted nothing to do with me.

I had also been struggling with self-worth issues and did not feel I was good enough for anything or anyone. This led to a continued abusive relationship that lasted for five years and worsened the terrible self-esteem I had created in myself. I had let this other person control how I felt and determine how I was going to live my life. I had given this person the reins to my future and I did not have the strength to take them back. At the time, I did not know any better and thought this was the life I was going to live forever.

It wasn't until that relationship ended and my best friend introduced me to my now-fiancé that I understood how much I deserved. I am stronger than I have ever been and I owe that to him. It is because of him I have been able to work through my issues and the questions that were raised after my dad's death. I now know my own worth and how I deserve to be treated. I understand now that sometimes we will never know the reason why; we have to trust in our faith that things happen for a purpose.

When I was twelve years old, I remember wanting to be a doctor or a professional basketball player. Those wants and desires have since drastically changed. At twenty-two, I have graduated college with a degree in social work and am still searching to find my purpose in this life. I just got engaged to the love of my life and could not be more thrilled to embark on this journey with the person who has encouraged me to be the best I can be. I strongly believe in the saying, "Everything happens for a reason," and I feel the struggles and situations I have been in throughout my young life have led me to the correct path God has chosen for me.

I continue every day to work on myself and figure out what I'm supposed to be doing.

My future plans are to enjoy my life with my future husband and hopefully start the family I have long dreamed of having. In addition to the medical issues with my father, I too have had my struggles. At the age of sixteen I was told that when the time comes to have children, I might experience great difficulty due to a condition called polycystic ovarian syndrome. This is something I struggle with every day but with my faith in God and the strength of my fiancé I am positive we will make this happen.

I am happy to be alive. So many people take their life for granted and it is something I have to remind myself of often. I am fortunate to have an amazing support system in my mom, fiancé, brother, friends, and family. The good relationships I have in my life are sometimes the only things that get me through the day. Knowing I have friends at work, friends out in the world, and a friend at home provides me the reassurance that I am doing something right. I pride myself in being an ear to listen and a shoulder to cry on for the people in my life.

Currently, wedding planning has become the "fun" thing in my life. It provides me the opportunity to connect with my mom, future mother-in-law, and future sister-in-law. It also gives me the opportunity to get to know my fiancé even more as we sit and talk, and more importantly, compromise on decisions, which gives me so much hope for our future. When I am not wedding planning, I am either hanging out with my dog, Bailey, working, or spending time with family and friends. I like to keep busy, so being able to find balance has been the latest challenge!

If I could go back and give my eighteen-year-old self some advice, I would say to not sweat the small stuff. I would say that people are going to hurt you and make you mad; they're going to do things you never thought another human being could do, but you have to push through. There are going to be very dark days, but there is a light at the end of the tunnel, and these experiences are going to make you stronger. I would tell myself I am worthy, I deserve to have great people in my life, and to never settle for less than I deserve.

Discovering My Light
Maddy Sevilla

When I was lying on the cold, dark cement after falling twelve feet in the air, something inside me changed. For the first time in my life, I was forced to question my long-perceived invincibility. Twenty-somethings do not typically give much thought to death. Most are born thinking they have a good century of life ahead of them. On July 12, 2014, I dived into the darkness. Consequently, my spirit was reborn and I saw the light for all its brilliance.

There is not much to do in the small town of Menomonie, Wisconsin, during the summer months. Most of the college students head home and a certain quiet charm is left behind. After a long day at work, some friends and I decided to utilize Wisconsin's resources and go grab a couple beers. Before we knew it, 2:00 a.m. had rolled around and we meandered on home. The Wilson Park amphitheater was no more than fifty steps away from my house. I had walked by this outdoor band shell almost every day and always admired its stature. On this particular day, I felt an overwhelming force pulling me up onto the stage. Maybe it was fate, or maybe it was the beers, but my little-girl instincts wanted me to dance across the stage like an actress straight out of Hollywood. As my friends laughed and goofed around amongst themselves, I spotted a green bench in the shadows at the end of the stage. It was the perfect place for me to jump up and showcase my talents for all to see.

It happened faster than the flutter of an eyelash. In an instant I understood how merciless gravity actually was. In my attempt to sit on the edge of the stage, I managed instead to hurl myself over the wall and slam the left side of my body onto the steps below. Time stopped. The pitch black made me question if I were still alive, but pain soon reminded me of my existence. They say when you have a near-death experience, your life flashes before your eyes. That didn't quite happen to me, but I was faced with a few revelations about my past.

The ambulance came to take me to the hospital and despite the blood covering my face, I still managed to flirt with the paramedic (my sense of humor seems to shine during inappropriate dramatic situations). I went back to my parents' house with one broken sinus bone, one fractured wrist, a torn ligament in my knee, and a bone bruise along my entire leg. My injuries were miraculously minor considering the circumstances. Although I was lucky to be alive, the mental and physical pain began to take its toll. After a few days, I sank into a depression. Flashbacks of falling filled me with fear. I couldn't shake the unfathomable feeling of being an inch away from death.

One night I was lying in my bed and tears slowly ran down my face. Once again I revisited the moment of lying there on the pavement. I asked myself, if the circumstances had ended differently, would I have any regrets? After pondering the question for a long while, I came to a conclusion. My only regret would be if my life had been taken from me that day in July, I would have died with too much love left inside me. Many people in my life would never know the true feelings of gratitude and admiration I felt for them. Too often I had let fear impede my abilities to express my love freely and wholeheartedly. Fireworks began to illuminate the darkness. I am not talking metaphorically; I am saying literal fireworks went off at that very moment. I wiped my tears and stared out the window in astonishment. It was a moment so magnificent it belonged in a movie; perhaps it should have been happening to the Hollywood actress I so longed to be. The best part was this was not a movie. This was real, and it was happening to me.

I began to slowly take control of my emotions, and spent the next month on the road to self-discovery. There was not much to do in my parents' house, and I was in no condition to go anywhere. After several weeks, I mustered up the strength to leave the house, but I wanted to go to only one place: Half-Price Books. I immersed myself in reading about spirituality and positive thinking. To this day, despite the pain I was in, sitting on the porch and reading those books were some of the happiest moments of my life.

It is fun to watch people's facial expressions when I tell them my fall was the best thing to ever happen to me. I consider this challenge to be the turning point in my life. Every person will experience a dark moment at one point or another. We must not drown in the sorrow of the darkness, but rather use it to truly appreciate the light that surrounds us.

Something marvelous happened when I changed my way of thinking. When I was younger, my greediness got the best of me. I wanted to experience intimacy in a selfish kind of way. I wanted others to shower me with the same love I denied myself. Now, I realized my desires have changed. Love is a gift that cannot be acquired. It can only be given, and in return, happiness takes its place. I have discovered love is a limitless resource that lives within myself. My hope is to inspire other young women to find this quality within them. We live in a culture that romanticizes the concept of lust. What it fails to teach us is that self-love is the soil in which all other love grows. When I changed my way of thinking, I began to shower my own soil with nutrients I desperately needed. By doing so, my relationships have bloomed beyond my wildest dreams.

Right now in my life I am happy to have embarked on my own spiritual journey. Perhaps it is my youthful optimism that gives me faith in the power of love. I like to think it is my choice to use every experience as an opportunity for growth that puts a smile on my face every day.

If I could give advice to my eighteen-year-old self, I would say you are never too young to die, and you are never too old to live. No matter what stage you are in life, there is always a discovery waiting to be made. Let the maps created by others guide you, but never let them dictate where you want to go. Do not be afraid to take risks and immerse yourself in the unknown darkness. Let your heart be a compass in your exploration and let it lead you to appreciate the brilliance of the light.

In Our Thirties

Live the Moment;
It's All We Have
Kristen Brown

L
ife has a way of throwing us curveballs when we least expect them. For the first part of my life, I was blessed with very little hardship or seriously painful experiences. I grew up in a middle-class family in a rural Minnesota farming community that was safe and gave kids many opportunities to try different things. That exposed me to so many things I couldn't decide what I liked most, so I just did it all. I was a busy person from my earliest years, always involved with or leading teams, committees and groups. This continued into my adult years as a go-getter at work, building my skills, leadership experience and exposure to various industries. I rose up the career ladder quickly, traveled the world, and made big money in the corporate world, all while hanging out with friends and eventually marrying a guy from my hometown whom I hadn't really known, but who'd lived just a few blocks from me growing up. Todd was my complement because he was laid-back and upbeat to balance out my serious and type-A tendencies. We had a daughter, Brooke, in 2006.

While life seemed pretty close to perfect, I was in for a reality check. It was the first big curveball I had ever been thrown. In 2007, Todd died unexpectedly of a heart attack in his sleep the morning after my sister's wedding. He was thirty years old and a tall, skinny, former college athlete. He had just been given a clean bill of health at a recent physical, making this tragedy even more shocking.

Losing someone so unexpectedly was not only the loss of the person, but the loss of my sixty-year plan. Our daughter was only ten months old at the time, and we owned a home and had a dog. Plus, I was in a high-pressure corporate leadership role with a new and challenging boss in the middle of an economic downfall. This created a stressful and scary situation in which I had no idea what to do or how to move forward. It was only through some serious soul-searching, education, and self-care that I was finally able to see the light again—and feel hopeful for the future, despite it being different from the sixty-year plan I'd had with Todd.

Not only did I write a bestselling book about my journey through widowhood, but it actually launched me into a new career as a speaker and bestselling author. I left the traditional corporate world and now serve it in my own way. This has given me the flexibility to spend time with my daughter and take care of myself so I can be healthy and strong for her. My future plans are all about honoring my own needs so I can be my best me and be the role model Brooke needs to grow up into a productive, happy, and healthy woman. And if there is another chance at love along the way, that would be great too!

I'm always the most joyful when I am contributing to the world in some way. Sometimes that is by spending quality time with my daughter so we can both spread happiness to others. Sometimes it is speaking on stage to audiences and helping them love their work and lives. Other times, it is when I sit in silent contemplation envisioning my next steps—those that will ultimately help others. That's what makes me happiest—and a good glass of wine or some bacon.

I am a huge movie buff and love a dark theater and a bucket of triple-buttery popcorn. Spending time with my daughter is my favorite thing to do, because no one makes me laugh like she does. And I love to eat!

If I had to tell my eighteen-year-old self something (and this is a big one for others, too), it would be to take care of your health, don't overspend, and really live in each moment. Don't worry so much about what's happening next—after work, this weekend, next month, when you retire. Instead, focus on the simple amazingness of this very moment...and then this moment...and then this moment.

It's all we have.

The Tenacious Thirties
C.E. Sawyer

There is certainly a psychological shift that happens from our twenties to our thirties. I may not look that much different, but the emotional growth is immense. I honestly don't recognize my younger self, and I don't think your twenties necessarily prepare you for the future. The twenties are about breaking free from the constraints of living at home, and chipping away the exterior to start to form the person you will become. The twenties lead to self-discovery, mistakes, and wild moments that create those "remember when?" stories. Where I'm focused today is vastly different. I was always goal-driven and motivated, but I think I'm more comfortable pursuing my personal goals and feel less influenced by societal and family pressures. I find there is a tenacity that comes with your thirties—a confidence that allows you to be more comfortable in your own skin.

The feeling of immortality seeps away after your twenties; parents are older and may go through various health challenges, and it can change a person's perspective. My father battled cancer, and one of my good friends committed suicide during college, creating big challenges for me. I feel now we are all here trying to do the best with the time we have, and helping those around us go through their journey becomes more important.

My wants and desires have definitely changed over the last ten years. I feel like I am a completely different person in my thirties than my early twenties, in a good way. I think it is easy to wrestle with who you *think* you should be and what you've been told you should strive for in your twenties, while in your thirties you are able to find your true self and you start to live more by your own definition of success.

Travel is important to me, and creating financial security for my family. We are building our financial portfolio so we will be able to live the lifestyle we envision for ourselves. That is the type of thing I would have never thought about in my twenties, but it feels good to have a plan and work towards personal and professional goals. In my twenties, I looked at my cousins and other family in their thirties and I considered it a "scary age:" a time of change, one that marked the end of an era of being young and carefree. Luckily, I found it's actually pretty exciting to be in my thirties. I feel more confident in my convictions, which has allowed me to take more control over my personal and professional decisions. It's an empowering feeling.

I find immense pleasure in finding purpose and passion in life, and for me, that centered on the creative process of writing novels. I am trying to dedicate as much time to my writing and career goals as I possibly can, and am not concerned anymore about society's standards of success. I realize this is my life; I get to make the calls, and life is too short to be anything but happy. You start to realize that time seems to go by faster as you get older, which makes me intent not to waste a moment. I figured out how I can give back and positively impact other's lives. I'm also less judgmental of myself. If I want to change something in my life, I have the power to make my life what I want it to be. I feel more in control of my future now than I ever have before, and I love the fact I see endless possibilities.

I used to think that having a nonstop social calendar equated to fun, but I'm realizing I'm the kind of person who needs time by myself to recharge. I value this downtime more than I ever have before, because I can focus on my hobbies and things that are important to me. My husband and I like to have quiet nights at home with our dog, which may have sounded boring back when I was in my early twenties. But now I find nothing beats curling up in front of the fire with a nice glass of wine and family. Most of my friends in their thirties own homes, so we have entered the time in our lives when entertaining at the house is more appealing than the late-night bar scene, and it can be loads of fun to host a grilling-and-game night.

I would tell myself at age eighteen to stop measuring myself against others' expectations. I know now the key is to focus on what will make you happy and the rest will follow. I am a strong believer that you can't reach your full potential being miserable. A happier you will make a more productive you, and if you find the perfect blend that makes you happy, you will be able to present your best self to the world.

I would also give myself advice about friendships. At twenty-one, you think you have made your best friends for life. You may be one of the few that keep those friendships forever, but I can tell you my original core group of friends, whom I thought would stay close, is down to a select few, and that's okay. The friends who are able to grow with you and support you through the years are the ones you will want to have in your life, and if others lose touch, don't get down on yourself or think you failed in keeping the relationship active. Friendships often form around key values and common interests. It is natural to change these relationships as you progress through life; your priorities in high school and college are most likely vastly different than in your thirties. Relationships will ebb and flow like tides in the ocean. It is natural, and key relationships will form and transform throughout your life in surprising ways.

Lifting Your Voice for Justice
Artika Tyner

The wisdom of my foremothers has prepared me for this period in my life. My Grandma Nellie was my first teacher. She taught me the importance of serving others and making a difference in the community. She lived out her faith by serving in the church and ministering to needs of "the least of these." I remember as a child watching her give clothes to those in need, serve meals to the hungry, and open her home to strangers.

Grandma Nellie also fostered my love of learning. Our weekly ritual was buying books at the local thrift store. Today, I still enjoy reading new books and learning new ideas and concepts.

My legal education has provided me with the tools for becoming an effective advocate for justice. From an early age, I recognized the law is a language of power. I needed to learn this language in order to ensure that my community had access to their rights and a voice to shape their destiny.

The biggest challenge I overcame was a fear of public speaking. In my younger years, I struggled with a speech

impediment. I often found myself excited to share my story
and insights, but stumbling over my words would get in the
way. This created a fear of public speaking, and over time I
buried my voice. While in law school, I resolved to become
a transactional lawyer in order to avoid speaking in the
courtroom. In my third year of law school, I was admitted
into the clinical program, in which we represented victims of
domestic violence. As I listened to the stories of my clients,
I realized my voice was important. Using my voice was
no longer a personal endeavor, but soon became a moral
imperative. I had an obligation to speak up and take a stand
against the injustices experienced by my clients. The words
of my grandmother were brought to my remembrance: to
whom much is given, much is accounted for. It was now time
to lift my voice for justice, and I have not been silent since.
Today, I am a civil rights attorney and my work focuses on
education and criminal justice reform.

I want to be more confident in who God created me
to be. Each day, we are tempted to compare ourselves to a
false image of perfection—the reflection of someone else,
or the persona of who others expect us to be. For a personal
example, I have worn a size eleven shoe since I was in sixth
grade. This poses a challenge for shoe shopping, since size
nine is the average shoe size for most females. I cannot tell
you how many times shoe sales clerks have asked me to try a
size ten or ten-and-a-half when my size is not available. Too
many times I simply agreed and bought the shoes that were
clearly too small in order to simply conform to someone
else's idea. I did not want to seem challenging; therefore I
accommodated the desires of another.

Fast forwarding to today, I learned that I am fearfully and wonderfully made, even when wearing my size eleven stilettos. I can no longer waste time focusing on *'who I think I should be*, or accommodating the needs, wants, and desires of others. Now, I focus on *who I was created to be*. I have taken inventory of my gifts and talents and discovered ways to leverage them to advance social justice.

For instance, my strengths are research, writing, and strategic planning. Each day, I use these skills to write for justice, lift my voice for justice, and create practical solutions to the pressing social justice issues of the twenty-first century.

In the future, I will continue the work of training and empowering the next generation of leaders and change agents. I will train students to serve as social engineers who create new inroads to justice and freedom. Additionally, I seek to build *Planting People, Growing Justice* leadership institutes across the globe to provide community members with the tools to develop their leadership capacity and influence public policy reform.

A quote posted in the South Africa Apartheid Museum inspired me to support education, entrepreneurship, and women's leadership initiatives in Africa. "A society attempting to develop without the participation of women is like a bird trying to fly with only one wing. It is bound to go off course."

I am happy with my circle of support, which includes my family, church family, friends, colleagues, and mentors. We spend time together uplifting and encouraging one another.

I enjoy traveling across the world, learning new languages, and baking. I travel internationally whenever I have a chance. I fondly recall my mother inquiring about why

I traveled so often to new places abroad. I responded with a smile and said, "Because I am a citizen of the world." Most recently, I traveled to Zhengzhou, China, where I taught in the World Academy for the Future of Women (WAFW). I was inspired by the exercise of leadership demonstrated by students who are committed to achieving the UN Millennium Development Goals.

In middle school, I began studying Mandarin Chinese. This provided me with the opportunity to learn about a new culture and build new cultural bridges. Each country I travel to, I try to learn a few new words. I am now studying Swahili to prepare myself for my next visit to Tanzania. The Swahili phrase, "*Hakuna matata*" (roughly translated, "No worries") has reminded me not to worry and cherish each moment in life. Also, during my visit to South Africa, I learned about a Nguni Bantu term, "*Ubuntu*," which means a person is a person through others. *Ubuntu* has informed my understanding of the very essence of community by which we have a shared humanity and common destiny.

Sweet treats bring joy to every occasion. I share this joy by baking my signature treats—Red Velvet Cake and Pumpkin Spice Cake.

I start each day with a mantra which provides me with the inner strength to be bold and courageous on life's journey. I would like to share three of my favorite motivational statements.

- **You are a gift to the world with immeasurable power to make a difference in the world.**
"Our deepest fear is not that we are inadequate. Our deepest fear is that we are powerful beyond measure. It is our light, not our darkness, that most frightens us.

We ask ourselves, "Who am I to be brilliant, gorgeous, talented, fabulous?" Actually, who are you *not* to be? You are a child of God. Your playing small does not serve the world. There is nothing enlightened about shrinking so that other people won't feel insecure around you. We are all meant to shine, as children do. We were born to make manifest the glory of God that is within us. It's not just in some of us; it's in everyone. And as we let our own light shine, we unconsciously give other people permission to do the same. As we are liberated from our own fear, our presence automatically liberates others." (Williamson, Marianne. *A Return to Love: Reflections on the Principles of a Course in Miracles*. New York, NY: HarperCollins, 1992.)

- **Don't follow the crowd, instead follow your purpose.**

  - People are often unreasonable, irrational, and self-centered. Forgive them anyway.

  - If you are kind, people may accuse you of selfish, ulterior motives. Be kind anyway.

  - If you are successful, you will win some unfaithful friends and some genuine enemies. Succeed anyway.

  - If you are honest and sincere people may deceive you. Be honest and sincere anyway.

  - What you spend years creating, others could destroy overnight. Create anyway.

  - If you find serenity and happiness, some may be jealous. Be happy anyway.

  - The good you do today, will often be forgotten. Do good anyway.

- Give the best you have, and it will never be enough. Give your best anyway.

- In the final analysis, it is between you and God. It was never between you and them anyway. (Found written on the wall in Mother Teresa's home for children in Calcutta, India)

• **Live out your faith. Christ has no body now but yours.**

No hands, no feet on earth but yours. Yours are the eyes through which he looks compassion on this world. Yours are the feet with which he walks to do good. Yours are the hands through which he blesses all the world. Yours are the hands, yours are the feet, yours are the eyes, you are his body. Christ has no body now on earth but yours. (Teresa of Avila)

Beyond the Comfort Zone
Meg Wrobel

I have had many wonderful experiences in my life as well as many learning experiences. Being the youngest child of seven in a broken home helped me become grateful for many things. My mother made my clothes, and the only time we received anything new was for Christmas or birthdays.

My early childhood was wrought with anger, fear, stress, and anxiety. I never really felt safe and wanted. I felt more like a burden on everyone, and this caused me to grow up very fast.

After I graduated high school, I was conflicted about what to do next. I didn't have parents who encouraged me to do anything, so I smoked a lot of pot, worked my butt off, and did nothing but drugs, factory work, and stagnation. A guy I went to high school with showed up looking all ripped, with a shaved head, and I was immediately interested in what he had been doing. Turns out he had joined the Marines. "The few, the proud." Yes, this sounded like a good idea for me. I had been a closet badass my whole life, and I thought, "What have I got to lose?"

Off to the recruiting center. Well, the Marines recruiter wasn't there that day, but the Navy guy popped out the second he saw me and stuck to me like a barnacle. Keep in mind, this was 2001 and September 11th had just happened. The Navy created a whole new rate (job) after this and needed thousands of people to fill billets of physical security on bases. At one time, Navy police were called shore patrol. Now they are called Master at Arms. A Master at Arms I became.

Boot camp night arrival: Just like Forest Gump, actually, screaming at you as you got off the bus, "Line up! What is your social security number? Move it! Double time! Don't look at each other. You're all ugly!"

Processing, humiliation, yelling; just pay attention, and whatever you do, don't *draw* attention! Bunk. Next day, supplies, uniforms, yelling, lines, order, pay attention! Once we got our sea bags, we filled them with everything we'd just received.

Boot camp was a long eight weeks. Some highlights were grueling. The abandon-ship drill was particularly memorable, seeing as how I was terrified of heights. I stood up on that platform shaking, and I didn't know how my body was going to leave that thing. Luckily, the kind gentleman up there in the incredibly short khaki shorts gave me a hell of a push when he sensed a slight hesitation on my behalf. My shriek echoed in the silent auditorium. Thank God, I could swim. I swam like crazy the second I hit the water and passed the test.

I left Great Lakes a sailor in the U.S. Navy. Next stop: A school where you go to learn your rate. In my case, boot camp number two: Military Police Academy. As I write this, I feel my blood pumping. I loved this! Riot control, defense tactics, collapsible batons, takedowns, arm-bars, clearing the room, pepper spray, grueling workouts, no excuses! I loved all of it and was first in my class academically. I also earned ribbons in shooting—expert pistol and sharpshooter in the M16.

After an honorable discharge, I found myself back home in Minnesota after being convinced by my mother to go to school for at Aveda Institute of Beauty and Wellness in their Esthiology/Skin Care program. I moved in with my older sister, got on the waiting list and started working as a waitress at a cocktail bar.

Into my life walked the man who became my husband, recruiting me with his handsome looks and business card. I did it; I called him the next day. As I've said before, I was clueless. We had a lot in common, including Navy service. Scott was a salesman. We got pregnant within about three weeks. *Bomb*! Life-changing event. The seas at this time were quite stormy, but we eventually decided to make a go of the whole relationship and raising a child together.

When our beautiful son, Aidan, was about eighteen months old, Scott drove himself to the hospital in the middle of the night. I received a call at three a.m. by a doctor saying I had better get there right away. Turns out he was in massive heart failure and as the doctor sat me down, he told me it was time to call in family. This was certainly another earth-shattering event. I cried outside the hospital room as a priest read him his last rights. Remarkably, with modern medicine and the best cardiologists in the country, after weeks in the hospital, he was pulling through. This opened our eyes to wanting to live healthier lives, and he recovered.

We got pregnant again with my sweet baby girl. Sophie was a very colicky baby, and I worked nights waiting tables. This was very hard for us financially, in the year 2008, when massive lay-offs were going on and my husband lost his job.

We had to be on every type of assistance possible.

I met a lady who introduced me to a machine for facials called "microcurrent." This technique would lift and tighten the skin and with a series of sessions, take years off your appearance. Scott and I believed in the results and we bought the machine. I set up a small office in our basement and started advertising on Craigslist. I was able to start making some money and we eventually moved into a small office in town and set up a real business. After a few months, I realized I was in the wrong location and found a new location off the interstate highway. There I worked with an acupuncturist who owned the building. My business really grew, and I stayed in a small one-room office for about a year. I met with the acupuncturist and we decided to create a med-spa, with acupuncture, microcurrent facials, yoga, and massage.

The biggest challenge I've ever had was trying to run a business with contractors. No one wanted to put in any more time than they were paid for. People wanted more and more from me, and I was breaking. I was also a mother with two young children, and the acupuncturist, whose grand idea it was to collaborate on this journey, was nowhere to be found. Somehow I found time during the night to work with Chinese manufacturers to produce airbrush makeup machines. I had perfected an amazing blend of airbrush makeup from several US labs and was doing very well with sales. I couldn't hold up the fort for everyone, though, and my meltdowns were becoming far too frequent, so I pulled the plug and walked away. I flushed $10,000+ in decorating, down the drain.

I found a small office hidden away and licked my wounds for about a year, bitter, angry, and resentful. I decided to go through a program of self-development called "The Six Advisors." This program opened my eyes to many of my shortcomings. Two of my greatest problems were general professional boundaries, and being passive-aggressive. I learned how to rethink and change some of my thought processes, leading to a stronger sense of self. Now I am in a large salon and my first-ever retail type of location with potential walk-in traffic. The only problem is, it's just me. I need to lock the doors while I do services and have very limited availability to attend to walk-in customers.

In the near future, I hope to make enough money to afford a receptionist, and I plan to find the perfect investor to buy my makeup line and give it much-deserved and needed promotion. I also have become obsessed with a network marketing product of nutraceuticals that have helped me get into the best shape of my life. This product has also shown me a much better way to earn money than the traditional business structure. It's the way to go, and my future plan is it.

Right now, I have two incredible children who are healthy, athletic, and desire everything out of life, and they are smart, caring, and beautiful. I also have a husband who, though we've had our turmoil, worships me and is very hard-working and always striving to better himself.

Fun for me is sitting on a patio in the sunshine with a glass of sauvignon blanc, or seeing my children play and have fun. I also love to crochet, knit, and exercise. I love to watch my body change when I fuel it with superfood nutrition.

Advice for an eighteen-year-old would be don't get credit cards, or at least have a general idea of how it works; yes, it is money you have to pay back. Don't be passive; say what you mean, mean what you say, but don't say it mean. Be grateful!

Most of your tragedies are nothing compared to the soldiers getting blown up overseas for our freedom, or the families at home who are constantly horrified about their loved ones' well-being. You must know what service work is to better yourself. Work hard, and be kind to people.

In Our Forties

Not Through with Me Yet
Neda Kellogg

In my twenties, I had to begin the journey of taking care of my mom. She was diagnosed with catatonic psychophrenia, which means she hears voices. I had already been without her because of the onset of the illness beginning for me at the age of twelve. I went through middle school and high school traumatized, yet highly functioning.

As I matured into an adult, I traveled the road of seeking the highest wisdom from family, friends, and random others who would share situations and circumstances I found myself experiencing. In seeking wisdom and guidance, I also yearned for connection to genuine people who could keep my taste for loving relationships bridged together from person to person. Through mastering various jobs, dead-end romantic relationships, ups and downs of sisterly friendships, and the mental struggle to understand why I didn't have a parent who seemed to really care about me, I have arrived at a period of my life that loves the Divine for always keeping me protected, grounded, and surrounded by other gentle souls who love deeply.

I was preparing in my twenties and thirties to be in a position to be a youth-comforting adult to so many young people who need transparency, guidance, and direction. The experiences of parental abandonment, stepparent dream-killers, and naysaying family and friends have prepared me to share with girls how to overcome and be the change they truly wish to see in the world.

My biggest challenge is still being overcome. Each day I awake I am reminded of how blessed I am to be able to humbly approach others because I am flawed. When trauma happens, there is a process to retraining the brain to experience its positive opposite. This takes damn near a lifetime of working at it.

My trauma has been the absence of my mother, who showed me at an early age the true meaning of unconditional love, before being taken away from me through psychological warfare. At this certain age, I am still healing daily.

Many days are better than others as I gain strength to accept things the way they are, but I will be a work in progress, ensuring that I check in with myself to see where I am along the journey of overcoming.

My wants and desires have changed over the last ten years. I grew up in a very strict home with my father and his wife. My dad was a great provider, so my standard of living has always been suburban-lifestylish. Having two sons, my desire has been to give them a similar lifestyle, but even better. The only problem is that before, I didn't know the importance of having a clear plan. Now I do, and am focusing on personally developing in areas that are critical to legacy-building. My wants and desires are more focused and legacy-stretching.

The wants and desires I currently have are those that can set examples for our youth and my peers so we can create the world we want to live in. We can have exactly what we ask for in our health, careers, social lives, emotional lives, academic lives, and ultimately in our financial and spiritual lives.

My future plans include being on track to become one of the world's next millionaires. I am positioning myself to become one of the next leaders in youth development through honing in on my purpose to empower youth to connect their reality to their dreams. I am currently accomplishing this through my intensive nonprofit ten-month mentoring program for girls and through my private coaching workshops, seminars, and keynote speaking engagements.

My life has been fulfilling and blessed through my relationship with the Divine. I appreciate where I am. I appreciate being guided to continually develop as a person, executive director, and life coach. I appreciate more being able to make decisions from calm, peaceful places. I appreciate finding love at an older, more mature place in life. I appreciate that my kids are amazing people and that they trust my direction. I appreciate that God is pleased with me daily as I open myself up to be used to bring my purpose to fruition.

I have fun by traveling and spending time with my loved ones. Comedy is my goal, daily, through taking time to be in present moments and laughing at the love of being alive. Finding humor in my days is soothing to my soul.

Know the two most important dates of your life: (1) your birthday and (2) the day you find your purpose. Once you find your purpose, educate yourself on the western world's economy and align your vision with being a wealth-

creator by taking your natural talent and helping fill a
need in the world. Do this while building relationships.
Relationships are everything. Our stories shared through
these relationships are what fuels us to keep going daily.
Don't complain about what you see; instead, be the change
you wish to see in your world.

Risk a Little, Gain a Lot
Cindy Koebele

I began working at a very young age in my parents' record store. At the age of twelve, I knew all of the duties required to run the store on a day-to-day basis and had a hand in helping with most of those tasks. Both of my parents worked, so my siblings and I learned to cook and clean for ourselves, and we had a list of chores we were responsible for. Having a childhood that encompassed responsibility and obligations was hard sometimes, but it has helped me in many ways. I was always very organized and detail-oriented, and my mom tells me she still finds my little lists and goal charts when she is cleaning out closets and boxes around her home.

I experienced severe bullying in elementary school. Instead of dwelling on the situation or the hurtful things said and done, I chose to focus on being successful at work. Working as a teenager was a huge influence to my overall work ethic. I started my first job at fourteen years old in a local drug store and then worked in a few restaurants. I was assistant manager by the age of sixteen.

As I got older and more confident climbing the ladder in the workforce, I was more prepared to handle this in the professional work world and to stand strong on my beliefs and abilities. Even today, when I face negativity from competitors in the industry, I focus on the things I can control. I am completely confident in my belief that amazing service for customers and staff members is always going be great for my business. Good things happen to good people, and when you are grateful and genuinely care about others, you will stay on your path to success.

When I was twenty-five years old, I moved to Switzerland for two years. I faced a lot of frustration and loneliness living and working in a foreign county and not knowing the language and geography. That experience shaped my character in many ways. I learned that pushing myself out of my comfort zone results in a more open mind, greater confidence, and a better understanding of the world and myself. Since that time, I have worked to push outside the boundaries of what I think I can do because I know it will enrich my life. This philosophy led me to start my own title company in 2007—a decision which has opened a world of opportunities to me. I most recently took my first steps toward a longtime dream of becoming a children's author by writing my first book about my family's beagle. Each time I take one of those uncomfortable first moves toward something that scares but intrigues me, I know I am unfolding more of my story. I've learned the real risk isn't failing, but not giving it a shot.

I'm extremely happy with my career and the success of my growing business. It's motivating to work with such a dynamic group of people who are driven to reach their goals. I love mentoring our staff in their career objectives and generating new ideas to implement and enhance our operations. My family life is a huge contributor to my personal happiness, and I'm so grateful. I have a wonderful husband and love spending time at home and with our mostly-grown children. As I write and publish my first children's book series, I'm learning to explore and create in new and exciting ways. The balance of fulfillment and challenge leaves me content with the many blessings I have, and yet open to all the possibilities the future brings.

I wake up every day eager for the opportunities that lie ahead. I plan to continue on this exciting path by building and growing my title business and writing and publishing more books. I believe the world needs more female leaders. I want to develop a stronger presence in the community through leadership roles, speaking engagements, and mentoring. I want to motivate and guide other women on a positive path toward achievement and success. I want to inspire them to reach, and not be discouraged by the bullies in their lives.

Life gets busier and busier, and even though the work I'm doing is enjoyable, I know it's important to take time away and slow down. I love traveling with my husband and experiencing new places and sights. We plan a great vacation every year in February, where we reconnect and recharge for another busy and prosperous upcoming year. When business is hectic, I unwind by cuddling on the couch with a good novel or watching a show that takes me elsewhere for a while. My friendships add so much joy to my life, and I spend a lot of time with my girlfriends, many of whom also work in the business. We plan a regular trip to New York together to bond, shop, see Broadway shows, and appreciate each other's presence.

If I could go back and give my eighteen-year-old self a piece of advice, I would say, "Don't sell yourself short."

I didn't realize many of my abilities and recognize my competitive nature until later in life. I wish I had known then to make choices that would open the world a bit wider and to believe I was ready for any challenge.

Things Change and We Change
Faith McGown

All of my experiences—good, bad, joys, sorrows, even my ridiculous mistakes—have prepared me for this time in my life. Once I got to my forties, things seemed to fall into place. Not that my life became perfect; not by a long shot. But the pieces seemed to fit. Experiences seemed to make sense. Where once things had seemed chaotic, the various aspects of my life juxtaposed without rhyme or reason, now harmony emerged.

My biggest challenges in life have been internal. My parents were teenagers when I was born and they weren't ready or well prepared to take on parenting, although they did their best and worked very hard at it. The things that I, as a mother, view as most important for parents to provide—self-esteem, love, support, encouragement, consistency, and stability—were not priorities for my parents. Unfortunately, my parents were consumed with keeping a roof over our heads and food in our bellies. As a result, I came to believe they didn't like me.

At about age six, I remember wondering what it was about me that was unlovable. I settled on the belief I was ugly, and I carried that with me until very recently (and still sometimes fall back into that mental place). That belief led to eating disorders, unhealthy relationships, and many other struggles. I'm not sure I've completely overcome that belief, but I have made great, very gradual progress. Today, I can honestly say I love myself and view myself as lovable. And I don't believe I'm ugly. I don't always see beauty when I look in the mirror or at a photo, but I am satisfied with who I am and how I look.

My wants and desires have indeed changed over the last ten years. My desires in my twenties were dictated by the expectations of others: college, homeownership, a "good" job, looking for a husband with whom to start a family. I never found the husband, but I did start a family when I had my daughter Grace at age thirty-one. Her dad and I separated when she was less than a year and it's been just the two of us ever since.

In my late thirties, I realized I wasn't living the life I wanted. I was working far too much at a job that paid well but brought too much stress and little fulfillment. I wasn't taking good care of myself. I wasn't eating as well as I could and I was overweight. I was very focused on things outside of myself—parenting, my social life, and making money. I had lost sight of who I am and, I think, didn't believe I had the capacity to prioritize loving myself. On my own and with a life coach, I spent a lot of time thinking about what is really important to me. As a result, I made a career change, lost the extra weight and today, taking care of myself is a top priority.

My plans for the future are to be happy, healthy, and live a life filled with love. Spending time with my fourteen-year-old daughter brings me tremendous joy, and I enjoy the kind, funny, and interesting young woman she is becoming. I look forward to continuing to support her development and nurture our relationship through her teenage years and into her adulthood.

My theme for 2016 is *love*. I am working to build a life filled with love—people I love, a job I love, activities and interests I love. It is only recently I have been comfortable voicing my desire for love in my life. My doubts around being lovable left me terrified to make love a priority. Thankfully, that has changed.

I honestly can't think of anything I'm unhappy with in my life right now. I am healthy and fit and I feel lovable. Being a mother to my daughter makes me incredibly happy and proud. I do work I enjoy. I'm not quite to the level of challenge and fulfillment I crave, but I'm moving intentionally in that direction. I also have great work-life balance. I am still single, but I feel as though I am becoming clearer about what I want, and I have options, as opposed to feeling alone.

Lots of things are fun for me. Laughing is especially fun; spending time with friends and some family (especially when it involves laughing); hearing Grace laugh or sing; listening to music and dancing; exercising/working out/running/walking; cooking when I have the time is fun; and bargain shopping/thrifting is fun.

When I was eighteen years old, I wish I had known that we're all simply doing our best to figure out this thing called life and find our place within it. Nobody has all the answers, and I believe those who think they do tend to be the most clueless. Life is a journey. There is no destination. Things change and we change. And that's not only okay—that's what makes it great!

Change + Adjustment = Success
Renee Usem

The experiences that prepared me for this point in my life are described in two words, change and adjustment.

When I was young girl, my Dad got a new job and we moved from California to Minneapolis, Minnesota, where we knew three people. This was difficult, because I had a great love for the ocean. We had lived only a few blocks away from it, and part of our daily activity was to spend time on the beach. When we moved from there, I was in deep mourning for the sea.

Our family had an interesting dynamic, with each playing a role but not connecting together. Discussing problems was not a strategy our family embraced. I learned to make the best of the situation and carry on. I turned inward to cope, primarily because I had no other choice. I didn't understand my feelings, but knew they were big. I did what I knew, which was to move forward and carry on. I became very active in extracurricular activities in high school with volleyball, yearbook, orchestra, and stage lighting. At an early age, I learned to draw strength from myself and figure out a solution on my own. I had experienced one of my first lessons about change and adjustment.

My life moved forward and I graduated high school and went on to college. The first year was not very successful; my classes focused on my weaknesses. This was a dark time and I was unsure how I was going to finish three more years. My first idea was to get a new perspective, chose classes closer to my interests, and stay calm. Peppered around my room were notes saying, "You can do it." This strategy worked, and my grades became straight As. I stepped into an area of study that was my passion, and I was able to change, adjust, and be successful.

A few years after I graduated from college, my boyfriend's job took us to New York City. I created an exciting life with career, marriage, social scene, and travel. I was able to change and adjust.

The next step was children. One year after our first child was born, the 9/11 attacks hit. We lived one block from the epicenter, and our home was contaminated with asbestos. After leaving our apartment to flee the attacks, we never returned. Our entire community of friends had been displaced as well. The life I had created had been taken away, and there was zero evidence of my footprint. We were refugees in search of a new life and finally settled back in Minneapolis to be close to family.

I am grateful for my experiences and the tool belt to manage change, adjust, and survive my life.

One of my greatest challenges has been setting clear boundaries. I believe this occurred for two reasons: one, not understanding my emotions, and two, living with the mantra,

"Be strong and carry on." I became a problem-solver for everything and was not clear about what was mine to solve and what to leave for others. I read a book called *You Are Worth It*, and the process of doing the exercises in the book helped me uncover this challenge. I am establishing healthy boundaries to create the life I desire.

Over the last ten years, I have moved into a space where I want to be authentic to who I am. My values lead me away from living up to the expectations of others. A quote that resonates with me is, "It's not the path that you are on that is important; it's how you walk through the fire that matters most." I think it is easy to close our eyes and ignore the pain life presents. Walking through difficult times with courage, truth and grace is what matters the most.

My future plans are rather open-ended, but the sky is the limit. I only see opportunities. My goal is to impact the world rather than climb up the ladder. I am in a position to rewrite my story, and this occurred because I have had the courage to change and adjust my life to make it the best for me.

What makes me happy is exploring the city I live in and learning about new ideas. I have an insatiable curiosity for everything around me. The arts, culture, food, and innovation really inspire me. My personal goal is to add something new to my day, every day. To further my exploration, I purchase two new magazines monthly to help broaden my view. When I am stuck or feeling off-center, it is important to find a new environment. This is when I head to the museum and become lost in the artists' points of view.

Describing what I do for fun is challenging, because it's constantly changing. Being outside in nature, walking with friends or family, biking, listening to a concert, or strolling in a garden are at the top of my list. My creative side comes out in my other love—cooking. The French Culinary Institute in New York City gave me a strong foundation to understand the science behind cooking. Now it is fun for me to create without a recipe and see what magic occurs. When cooking for my family or friends, I am mindful of the experience they will have. The menu is created around their personalities and what would be interesting for them to experience.

My creativity extends into how I share my view of the world with my children. Each day, I try to expose them to something new, whether we take a new route to school or experience an adventure in the city. It is important to take time to see your environment from a new perspective and live life every day.

If I could give my eighteen-year-old self advice, I would tell her three things:

1. When someone shows you who they are, believe them the first time," (widely attributed to Maya Angelou)

2. Listen to how a situation makes you feel and respond to your internal alarm.

3. Be your authentic self and continue to discover new things to feed your soul and make you an interesting person.

In Our Fifties

Thrive
Amy Kennedy Fosseen

I understand every experience I've had has led to this place in my life, and I am the sum of all of them. Of all my experiences that have prepared me for this time in my life, the first ones I thought of were the hard ones: parents' divorce, moving, child cancer, my divorce, losing custody, death, running away—the list goes on. But the good ones have prepared me just as well: loving parents, family, friends, moving, love, children—this list goes on as well.

We all have challenges in our lives and I'm no different. Often the one we're going through at the time seems like the biggest. My two older children have both been addicted to heroin. My daughter has been clean for two years, and my son is on his fifth round of treatment. So, perhaps "overcame" is the wrong word—I'm moving through it actively. I believe this time, because my son and I are both working through this with group and private counseling, that we will both come through the other side, healthy.

I used to be so fixated on what I wanted to do (someday I'll finish writing a book, someday I'll go to France, someday I'll be rich and won't have to work). I'm not looking to "someday" anymore, nor am I looking to "doing" specific things. Right at this time my, desires are two-fold and family-focused: I want all my children to be healthy and happy and full of dreams; I want my husband to be healthy and happy, and I want the rest of my family to be healthy and happy. Do I have control over these things? Probably not. My other desire is to help women become—just that. Become more at ease, more playful, more inspired. I still have dreams for myself (I mean, it's *France*, people!) But if I can make one person feel better every day, or inspire them to make a change, then I've made a difference.

Sometimes I think my desires could become something in the future. I have this passion to help people, so I write a blog (that in the future, might become monetized), and I believe in holistic health, so I use and teach classes on essential oils (that in the future could make me some money), and I have a desire to travel, so I dream about traveling (which doesn't get me anywhere). And then I think, "Who cares about the future? What about right now?" So right now, this moment, I am ready for anything fabulous and will continue to do what I'm doing.

All of which ultimately makes me happy to be in the here-and-now. And, even though there are challenges in the here-and-now (as there will always be, whether huge or tiny), I can be happy.

I just heard this the other day: "Challenges are inevitable; suffering is optional." I always make the choice to walk beside my challenges or sadness. I choose to walk in happiness because I have so much to be happy about. I am so happy to be living the life I am living! My husband makes me laugh every day; my daughter is an inspiration to me constantly (plus she's magic); my son, in treatment, makes me so proud and he always tells the truth; and my youngest is my touchstone—he lets me know when I'm not being me. My mom has always been my hero(ine) and I am so happy that she is my mother.

Happiness has become my fallback option, but having fun is another matter. I think anyone can choose happiness; fun takes work! I believe in fun—fun at home, fun at work, fun for no good reason. Lately, I've tried to say "Yes" to more things; things like spending time with people I love, parties, playing cards—you get the picture. I believe laughter fixes our hearts, or, at least, mends them.

When I think about all my experiences (good and bad), the challenges of now, the great things happening, and my desires for the future, I wonder; if I could tell myself anything at eighteen to steer myself in a certain direction, would I? And what would I say? I think I would say, "Listen to your heart, not the people around you. You know what to do." Also, "Spend more time with your dad, write more letters, swim more often, choose friends over boys, and *go to France*." But I wouldn't say a word about anything else. I firmly believe we are always where we are supposed to be.

Fifty Shades of Life
Ann LeBlanc

My experiences have been good, bad, and ugly. I'll start with the good and the best experiences in my life. What is on the forefront of the good and best is becoming a mother. I do know love, unconditionally.

The tougher parts of my life pretty much boil down to loss. Loss came in the form of loss of friends, loss of family, loss of family life, and along the way, loss of me. Some of these losses felt bigger than life. I have learned some things along the way.

I'd like to think this is how I've settled into myself and what I believe—three things (not in order).

- **Number one: pick your fights.** I think I've learned this one mostly from observing other people. Some people are just happy being unhappy about everything. Choose what you want to complain about, argue, or stick up for, and take everything else with a grain of salt.

- **Number two: forgive yourself.** I learned this one on my own. I believe that all people make choices based on what they know at that point or where they are in that moment.

- **Number three: don't judge.** There are always two sides to every story. Most times, we tend to only get one view or an ear to one side.

The biggest challenge I have overcome was ending my first marriage. My twenty-one year marriage had been over for many years, but we remained together for many reasons. Finances and children not yet out on their own were our reasons for remaining together, but the real reason why we remained together was fear. My husband at the time wanted to stay together until our youngest son was in college. I was very much alone in this marriage. Being alone with someone is much worse than living alone.

I decided I wanted to end the marriage sooner rather than later. With that decision, I became the spouse to blame for the end of the marriage from his point of view. I knew this was far from the truth. After my husband and I separated, I decided to move. I moved halfway across the country from the town where I was born and raised all my life. Chapter two of my life started.

My wants and desires have changed in a couple of areas. I think I want less. I no longer want a big home with a big yard. I don't want to live in suburbia. I value fewer, but stronger, friendships. I still want to look younger, look good, and feel good. I hope that never changes!

Regarding future plans, for the near-term, I will be walking the *Camino de Santiago*, a 500-mile walk across northern Spain. I was able to walk a short portion of the *Camino* last year and am looking forward to walking it with my husband. Longer-term, I hope to give up a career in corporate America. With that change, I want to travel more with my husband, and I hope to have some work involving cooking.

I am so happy in my new marriage and in love with my husband of three years. I am happy with having his family in my life. I am also happy with my children as adults; I am happy in my relationship with them.

For me, having fun includes the following:

- Spending time with my husband
- Playing cards
- Spending time with my sons
- Exercising, including barre, yoga, and spin
- Cooking and hosting dinner

Knowing what I know now, if I could go back to give myself a piece of advice when I turned eighteen, I would say, "Be bolder, stand strong, and never be afraid."

Lessons in Fear
Georgine Madden

Nothing can prepare any of us for the vast emotional landscape we experience through the ages and stages of life. Most would probably agree that deeply feeling emotions like confidence, appreciation, love, and playfulness is a lot more appealing than diving into emotions like jealousy, betrayal, envy, and fear.

I used to think of my feelings as good or bad until I realized that labeling a feeling as "bad" influenced me to resist it, deny it, or blame someone for it. And feelings are undeniable. Our experiences in life bring them all to the surface and create the adventure life becomes.

My life experience took me on a deep-dive into fear. Here is my story.

It was 3:30 on Tuesday afternoon, April 20, 1999. My consulting career was taking off and I was working from home doing final edits to a leader-training guide for a big client. Life was feeling good—abundant and secure, when the phone rang. The woman on the other end of the line introduced herself as a coworker of my sister. She said, "Something really bad has happened." For a moment I know my heart stopped beating, and I asked with certain dread, "Has something happened to my sister?"

"It's Cally Jo. She's been murdered."

Cally Jo—my sister's daughter.

Like a computer glitch, my brain simply stopped processing. It was blank and silent, trying to put this foreign data together.

The voice on the other end jarred me back, "Your sister needs you to come down here immediately."

I heard myself say, "Okay, I'm on my way. Where should I go?"

"Everyone is on their way to the hospital."

Then I hung up.

Once at the hospital, I entered a room designated for families. There were four people in the room, including a pastor—a man I would later come to know as one of the most compassionate, caring, and generous people I know. He had a blank stare on his face. The others were my sixteen-year-old niece and two of her friends. My niece was the first to find Cally Jo. All three were in shock.

As time unfolded, I learned what had happened. Cally Jo, a vibrant, joyful, twelve-year-old girl, had come home from school to do homework before heading to her gymnastics class. On this day, she had come home to an intruder in the otherwise empty house.

To this day, I cannot imagine how terrified she must have been as the horrific acts unfolded. My heart ached with a pain I never thought possible. The newspaper headlines revealed enough: "Cally Jo Larson—cruelly raped and murdered by an intruder bent on burglary."

Over the next two years, I walked with my family through deep grief and posttraumatic stress. Eventually, the murderer was identified, tried, and sentenced to life imprisonment.

As a ripple effect, my children lost their innocence that day too. My sons were ten and seven at the time, and I moved them into our bedroom to sleep with us for months afterward. I needed to have them near me, especially in the silence of the night. It wasn't until we got our beloved dog, Sandy, three months later, I felt some solace in having them sleep in another room.

One evening, when we were reading stories at bedtime, my youngest son said, "I have a great idea! We can get bars for our windows so that no bad guys get in."

Once again, my brain froze, and I found myself replying, "What a great idea. And our house is made of bricks, so I don't think any bad guys could blow it down or get in." The look on my son's face made me realize I had said the thing he needed to hear in order to face his own fear.

This experience has given me a better understanding of posttraumatic stress, and I've experienced it many times over the years since. One day was five years later, when my youngest wanted to ride his bike to a friend's house to play. I felt the grip of fear on my heart, even though the friend's house was just eight blocks away. I knew cognitively he was responsible and capable of this journey. And I had done an immense amount of therapy that allowed me to observe my emotional reactions. I gave him a cell phone and told him to call me when he arrived and again when he was heading home. Then I took a deep breath, forced a smile and said, "Have fun!"

He was off and I busied myself with mindless activities around the house—cleaning the kitchen from breakfast, checking my email, dreaming up new crafting projects. I decided to take our dog for a walk to the park. Then I heard it. Screams from a young boy, a van door being slammed shut, and silence. Fear gripped me and I raced back to the house to call my son.

He answered immediately. "Oh, sorry Mom. I'm here. I forgot to call you. I'm having fun!"

I have known many faces of fear; fear in walking to my car in the parking ramp, fear of entering my empty house, fear that my health will fail, fear that my business won't produce, fear that I'm not good enough, fear that I can't make it on my own, fear that I'm not loveable, fear that I will succeed and not be able to handle it—the list goes on and on.

Though the years, however, I've learned to observe my life experiences from a different perspective and deeper consciousness around human fear. It doesn't make the emotional experience of it any easier, but it does provide some balance. I have learned to manage the polarity of fear and security. Now, fear elicits in me a motivation to be conscious and mindful of the choices I'm making. I've learned to stop judging myself for having fear, because we all have it, which gives me more compassion for others.

Fear, in whatever form it shows itself, is a part of all of us. I'm not afraid of fear anymore. I see fear as a shadow. It is always with you. And when it appears, I look for the light that is also shining within me, calling me to focus on the best of who I am.

I find amazing wisdom in this quote from the founder of Agape International Spiritual Center, Michael Bernard

Beckwith: "Behind every problem, there's a question trying to ask itself. Behind every question, there's an answer trying to reveal itself. Behind every answer, there's an action trying to take place. And behind every action, there's a way of life trying to be born."

Looking back on my life, I wish I could have told my young self, "You will find richness in the depth of feelings. Don't be afraid to feel all of your feelings in the deepest way. You will find freedom there."

Gaining Momentum
Ellie Peterson

Taking the time to learn who I really am has enabled me to embrace life's precious moments. Therapy, meditation, creating and practicing Meditative Movements, journaling, reading self-help and spiritual books, being open to what life wants to teach me, and exploring nature have all prepared me for this time of my life.

The biggest hurdle I've overcome was my divorce at the age of twenty-three, and the challenge of single-parenting my five-, three-, and one-year-old. As Ellie from the deli, making eighty dollars a week, I struggled financially. My physical health was burdened with smoking, a negative body image, and a sedentary lifestyle. My feelings of unworthiness, helplessness, and fear created the most difficulty. When I learned about my own personal power and started exercising it in healthy ways, change slowly started to occur in me. Understanding the nature of life and how to be calm and peaceful with my life experiences has allowed me to be happy and feel whole.

My main goal—to be healthy—has not changed over the past ten years. What *has* changed is that I want to give and receive freely instead of thinking of getting. To be open and experience life without fear goes along with this notion. Complete trust. This requires conscious effort on my part to be aware, and then the willingness to change my perspective when it is misaligned.

For more than thirty years, my dream has been to share the Meditative Movement technique with others. I've dabbled in making this dream a reality. Four years ago, I decided to focus all my work energy on building a business. I left my corporate life where I'd made more than six figures a year, loved the profession, and was in a comfort zone; that is gone. It's been replaced with new challenges and lots of personal growth. Because I want to enjoy all of my life, I have created a healthy balance of taking care of me, spending time with family and friends, then making time for work.

My husband and I purchased a condo in Florida last year, so my plan is to be a Minnesota snowbird for six months of the year. Meeting new people and establishing a social network is exciting.

Growing the business through speaking engagements, certifying others to teach Meditative Movements, and creating new products and services that meet our customers' needs is high on my priority list.

Writing is a passion. I find so much enjoyment in letting the words flow, and I will share my insights through published articles, books, and social media outlets.

A new hobby is watercolor drawing. Learning to play an instrument (maybe the piano) will be happening soon. I've practiced on the library's piano after viewing YouTube videos and reading books on the subject. Perhaps it's time to start taking formal classes.

Several years ago, I took sailing lessons. One goal is to be part of a crew and sail on the open waters for a couple of weeks.

At some time, I would like to live in France for a couple of years. I speak the language and during college spent two weeks there. While visiting a country is nice, living there and getting to know the citizens is a totally different experience.

There are so many blessings. My relationship with myself makes me the happiest. As I become more in tune with life's intricacies, I feel liberated. Once I become aware of past hurts and fears, I am able to forgive and let go. Yes, sometimes I struggle, yet I have been practicing for so long, I'm getting quite good at it. Continuing to be aware of myself and loving myself unconditionally are key components to my happiness. Living in the present moment offers me peace.

The ease with which I spend my days is appreciated. I wake up without an alarm clock, spend time meditating, journaling and reading inspirational material first thing in the morning. Then I enjoy my latte and a croissant with fruit for breakfast. Spending a set amount of time on business then going off to lie by the pool, visit the grandkids or go to a sporting event is exhilarating. Living downtown offers me the opportunity to walk or ride my bike to meet clients, teach classes, and attend networking events.

Having a healthy relationship with my other family members comes in second.

Being called grandma is music to my ears. It is so much fun to be with my six grandchildren and my own grown children. Playing Alfred, the butler, with four-year-old Batman Charlie is a highlight.

It brings me great pleasure to visit our local museums and points of interest. For example, once when meeting my daughter in St. Paul, Minnesota, we were too early for happy hour. Walking around, we happened upon the Landmark Center, where we listened to young musicians playing their instruments, then explored the Schubert Club Museum and the Gallery of Wood Art.

Every year, I participate in a different type of meditation retreat. Visiting different places of worship opens my mind and reminds me of the vastness of thought.

During the summer, riding our bike trails is amazing. My favorite ride has me stopping at the Depot Coffee House in Hopkins to listen to a musician play on his keyboard as I eat a peanut butter brownie.

Traveling domestically and abroad offers many rich experiences. It warms my heart to learn another culture, even if that means taking the Amtrak through South Dakota.

Advice I would give to someone at age eighteen would be to believe in yourself and trust life. The gift of life is precious; appreciate and experience every moment.

In Our Sixties

Rediscovering U
Barb Greenberg

The phone call came at three o'clock a.m. There had been a car accident. Our younger college-age daughter, who was exploring the world with three friends and a backpack, now lay in coma on lifesupport. My husband and I needed to get to the hospital immediately. We called the airlines and packed our bags. The phone call came from the Royal Brisbane and Women's Hospital in Brisbane, Queensland, Australia.

The seemingly endless flight took us from Minneapolis to Los Angeles, California, where we waited to take another flight from Los Angeles to Sydney, Australia, where we waited to take yet another flight from Sydncy to Brisbane.

It was late at night when we arrived in the ICU, and the lights were dimmed. Our daughter was surrounded by beeping machines and attached to tubes that kept her breathing, drained her damaged lungs, eased the pressure on her brain, and monitored her heart. The doctors did not think she would survive, and if she did, they felt she would have severe brain damage.

I instinctively and immediately dug a trench deep in my heart from which I would fight for my daughter's life.

I believed she had already decided to return to us, whole and strong, and after ten days in a coma and two surgeries, that is just what she did, valiantly earning her title: "The Minnesota Miracle."

One month later, accompanied by a nurse, we returned to Minneapolis, where our daughter went directly into a nearby hospital. Soon she was home, returning to the hospital for outpatient therapy only, and then she courageously charged back into the world.

The crisis was over.

I collapsed into myself, unable to function, napping on the sofa for hours. A gentle therapist diagnosed me with depression. She decided not to put me on medication, instead saying my body was wiser than I was, and if I needed to lie on the sofa, that's just what I should do. So that is where I stayed, not moving, simply noticing my life, and what I noticed broke my heart.

My husband's behavior, which I wanted to believe was stress-related, was all too familiar. I ached to admit it had been there always. Raised to be a "nice girl," it had been my responsibility to find the good in people, giving them the benefit of the doubt, so I had consistently made excuses for him, for me, for us.

But from my vantage point on the sofa, I could see being a nice girl had not been enough to keep me safe. I don't remember when I had stopped offering opinions or sharing feelings. I didn't recognize the point at which I no longer trusted myself, but it was clear I was disappearing, fading like an old photograph. If I did not act soon, there would be nothing left of me. It was time to admit self-worth is non-negotiable, and deserting myself in order to maintain a relationship is not acceptable.

I had watched my daughter fight to reclaim her life, and it was time for me to do the same. After more than thirty years of marriage, I filed for divorce. We retained attorneys and sold our house. I moved into a small apartment, expecting to feel excruciatingly alone—and instead felt the safest I had in years.

In this space, I was able to tend the flood of raw emotions. Tremendous sorrow washed over me, and rage crashed around me. I struggled to make it through each day, exhausted and doing my best not to drown. In the midst of this swirling chaos is where the healing began, and with it came glimmers of hope.

Choosing to use my experience to make a difference for other women, I wrote two books and offered sporadic workshops to help others move through the process of divorce. A workshop now and then was all I thought I was capable of. I did not have the confidence or the vision to do more until a dear friend told me I had found my soul's purpose, and I decided to believe her.

Timidly, one small step at a time, I began to build my workshops into a company: Rediscovering U, LLC. The "U" represents the University-styled focus on educating women, with classes taught by top experts in the areas of divorce and healing. "Rediscovering" was chosen because, as painful as the divorce journey can be, it is a journey that allows you to rediscover your voice, your spirit, and ultimately yourself.

Of all the goals I had set for myself over the years, building a company was certainly not one of them. But the women

I work with inspire me daily and have built my confidence, broadened my vision, and given me the determination to grow Rediscovering U into a premier resource for women dealing with divorce, so no woman feels lost or alone.

My biggest challenge is to trust my path, trust I am being led where I'm meant to go, trust myself and my abilities, and have faith everything will unfold in its time.

My work is a joy. It's creative, meaningful, and challenging. And to have more fun, all I need is to meet a friend for lunch, take a walk, sit at a coffee shop and write, or get lost in a good book. A visit with my healthy, happy, out-of-town children and grandchildren raises the bar to a whole new level of joy and gratitude.

In the evening, when the cat curls up on my lap, I whisper to my younger self to *trust*. Trust, because it is often the most painful experiences in life that will be the best teachers and offer the greatest growth. Trust that when you feel lost, you can rediscover yourself by looking deep into your heart. Trust you will make it through even the darkest of times to find the path leading you to your life's purpose.

Reclaiming My Soul
Louise Griffith

We are all products of experiences life has provided, both positive and negative. The key is learning from all.

An event that changed my life forever was the divorce of my parents when I was fourteen years old. I was angry, devastated and fearful about how my future would unfold. At first, I did not tell any of my friends because I was embarrassed and ashamed. None of their parents were divorcing. I felt very alone.

My mother was extremely stressed due to the financial implications for our family and the emotional trauma of setting out on her own with no financial backup. She had been married for twenty-five years and spent twenty-three of those years at home raising five children. Therefore I, too, was worried and knew this was going to affect me and my future in a big way. Being a normal teenager who was mostly concerned about herself, I had very little compassion for my mother or for her situation. I do now. I see her as an extremely brave woman who had the courage and wisdom to honor her own soul at that time in her life.

I knew I would have to make my own way because money was so tight in our family. I began working at age fifteen. I always worked very hard to make the most of my education and paid my way through private high school and college with the help of scholarships. I therefore learned to be resourceful and independent as I pursued my own dreams and goals while needing to both survive and thrive.

School was important to me, as well as wonderful friends whose parents also welcomed me into their families and believed in me. Through their love and emotional support, I learned to be resilient. My faith in a loving and benevolent God also sustained me, giving me the hope as well as the belief I would be shown the way. I was also willing to do my part. I realized I was the only one who could be in charge of my attitude and be responsible for my choices and actions, which has served me well.

At age twenty-three, I got married. My future husband told me he loved me, and I thought I loved him. The relationship worked for a while.

Over the years, I was dedicated to doing all I could do to have a happy family. I thought that could happen if I just worked harder.

During that time, I was also paying attention to opportunities that showed up, such as pursuing a master of arts in counseling psychology, speaking as a profession, and certification as a success coach, all of which were a part of my soul's purpose.

This also allowed me to contribute to my family financially and provide opportunities for them that may not have been possible otherwise. This gave me great joy. Family was always my primary concern. During this busy time, I really didn't pay much attention to my soul. As I look back, I am reminded I was again being led, and certainly ignored many red flags at the same time.

In the process, I put myself at the bottom of my own list of priorities. Sometimes I wasn't even on my own radar screen. This was not life-giving to me, nor was it good modeling for my children. I let this happen very slowly. As a result, I gave away and lost who I was as a whole person.

Life changed with age, different job experiences, and stressors, as did the dynamics of my relationship with my husband. I made the decision to quit overfunctioning to make everything right, which had become a pattern in my life. I felt we had shifted from being collaborative partners to being roommates. Our needs were not being met or honored by each other. I came to realize this relationship was not based on mutual respect, trust, and love. There was not enough connection to sustain the relationship any longer. I acknowledged to myself the relationship had not been working for me for some time. It was not an easy decision, nor one made lightly.

The biggest challenge in my life was ending my marriage of forty-three years—making this hard decision because my soul was dying. Just as I knew my life would never be the same after my parents' divorce, I knew my life would change in many arenas—including my relationship with my children and grandchildren.

There are times in life when your path becomes clear and you know you must take that action. You really do have to listen to your inner self, your inner guidance, your soul.

Even though I had no details of how I would make it on my own at age sixty-six, it seemed I had done this before.

At some level, I knew many others may not understand. However, I needed to claim myself as a whole person. I realized it was my right and responsibility to take charge of my life. I had faith that once again, I would be shown the way. It was at this point I came to understand and respect my own mother at a deeper level.

I do have my energy back and am more connected to who I truly am. My decision to leave and my healing process were enhanced by my relationships with loving and trusted friends—friends who had traversed this ground themselves. I embraced opportunities to learn from workshops, an excellent therapist and several great coaches.

I am grateful for the joy and peace I feel within my soul. I know I have great value as a human being and also know I am worth it. I am passionate about helping others claim their own worth and value through speaking, coaching, and writing.

My second book is bubbling within me, even though I do not have specific details at the moment. Developing new products and programs to support my work is exciting to me.

At this point in life, I am more grounded and ready to grab life with both hands. I am less likely to "offer it up" and more likely to seek joy, whether it is being in nature, relationships, experiences or new learning.

Creating new memories with my two children and five grandchildren is at the top of my list. I look forward to spending more time with them and getting to know them more deeply as the magnificent human beings they are. Family is still one of my highest priorities. This time, however, I will be honoring my own soul as we grow together in a newly defined family that respects our individual and collective journeys.

The advice I would give myself as I turned eighteen—and again every time I am faced with change or a challenge in my life—is:

- Pause and be open to all opportunities, personally and professionally.

- Seek good, healthy mentors.

- Check inside of yourself to honor the wisdom already within you.

- Love yourself and love others.

- Know the gifts you have and share them with others.

- Pay attention to yourself, your circumstances, and to your soul.

- Be grateful often.

Most importantly: You are enough. You have great worth and value as a human being. You are a blessing to others. We all have to remember we are all doing the best we can at each moment. As Maya Angelou says, "We do what we know how to do and as we know better, we do better."

Just Hanging in There Wasn't Enough
Judith Milton

To begin, this period in my life is two-plus years after retiring from a nursing career I loved, in addition to utterly having changed my location, community, lifestyle, and health. Not a bad start in defining my "current period." Without going into all the details, I can tell you it's been quite a ride!

I arrived in this new place after selling off my house, boats, furniture, and everything most of us consider stabilizing items. Don't get me wrong. They *are* calming and stabilizing, these things. The problem was I was terrified by the thought of settling down into a nice, calm, retired life. Freaked out, indeed, *and* all alone.

So I arrived. Great. Now what? Never been here, didn't know one soul, had no idea *where* I was, exactly, or why in this place over any other. I was suffering from debilitating pain and other conditions, now recognized to have been stress-related, but crippling nonetheless.

All in retrospect now, my preparations for this period in my life were these:

- I'd done it before. In 1991, when I was forty-five years old, I sold everything, bought a boat, and went to sea for five years. (*Not* alone. I'm not *that* crazy.) I sailed all over the world, had amazing experiences of every imaginable kind, then returned to resume my life and career—which was harder than leaving it, believe it or not. I struggled to repatriate myself, but eventually reacquired all the stuff of a "normal" life. I was happy, got my friends back, relearned things like *never ever look at strangers or make eye contact with passersby nor touch other people's babies*, etc. It took years for this re-entry process to succeed, but I did it.

- This next bit confuses me. My parents, though adventurous and supportive of my adventure, were stable and loved their homes and their stuff. After all, they'd had each other for a lifetime, and I had saddled myself with thirty-eight years of the single life after eleven years of marriage in my youth. Prepared? Ha! I don't think so.

Folks: I am doing it. I'm thriving, I feel alive and happier than I've ever been. Sixty-eight years old and feeling like thirty-five. I have surrounded myself with amazing new people who have adopted me like their long-lost sister. I even seem valuable to *them*. I look forward to each new day because *absolutely anything* can and *does* happen to me. Incredible things. I feel like I might burst were I to be any more delighted with life. Go figure!

So this is what I now have to say about, "What prepared me for this period in life?" It is some kind of uncanny faith in myself and in life that I must have been taught along the way or learned by the seat of my pants. (I'm not religious, so that can't be it.) Perhaps it's because I have finally incorporated the values that are important to me and am able to sift through people's personalities until I locate the important ones. (Sorry, I insist upon it.) Time is galloping faster than I could have ever imagined in my youth.

Maybe we can agree to be comfortable with the mystery?

(It occurred to me just now the whole thing may have been a setup. I set myself up with challenges that leave me no choice but to change in order to survive. Just as everyone seems to know the really big events in our lives compel us to make the choice to fight and grow or to cringe and hide. Wow! I must be a difficult case.)

As we all hopefully know by now, *myself* is the answer to the biggest challenge we need to overcome. We (and life) present ourselves obstacle after obstacle, tripping and fumbling over each one. For me, they include (I'm *not* giving you the whole list):

- Fear that I won't be up to the challenges. I am forever forgetting the task may be really, really *hard*, and it's not that I'm too incompetent, weak, and stupid to accomplish it with speed and grace.

- Really terrible (not just whining) chronic pain and a host of other blocks. These obstacles I can say proudly I fought and scratched my way through and can now say, "I won," "I can live with that," or, "Screw it. I don't care anymore."

Regarding my wants and desires changing, that's funny. I was prepared to say, "Of course they have. What a silly question." I began to rummage through my "Brain of a Certain Age," and found the old mental list up there.

No. Not much change. I still want to stay young at heart. I want adventure and it matters not too much of what kind. I want dear friends, entertaining television, fun, and enough money to *have* said fun. I insist my grown children are sorry for everything they did wrong in adolescence (they are allowed to wait to confess until they're at my deathbed). I want them to be happy, keep staying out of jail, and above all else, to be safe. I want to feel I am giving of myself. I want a man to love, but I leave that to fate.

As the Spanish toast says, "To health, love, and money and the time to enjoy them."

All of the above make me happy right now. At this moment, beside world peace, (I practice spelling w-o-r-l-d backward and still can't do it) the end of misery and hunger, etc., I have all I've ever wanted at my fingertips. I admit that I am waiting for the other shoe to drop, but never in my life have I been this happy, for so many consecutive weeks and months.

(Keep this between us, because I know the gods of despair are in charge and would want to teach me a lesson.)

I am really proud of how I have fun: I simply make myself available for fun. I almost never turn down a chance for it with others, and I am almost always enjoying the moment while alone. If I am not having belly-laughing fun, I make a few calls and order some up from the Fun Menu of Life.

Advice for my eighteen-year-old self would be, "Get ready, little one. It's going to be a wild, wild ride. Proceed to the route. You're fine!"

Entering Unchartered Territory—for Me
Colleen Szot

In a few weeks, I will be sixty-three years old. Nothing has prepared me for this stage of my life—nothing. I still feel like a thirty-year-old career woman, making my way in the world. The saying goes that if I had known I was going to live this long, I would have taken better care of myself. In my case, that couldn't be more true.

My mother retired at age sixty-three. She had worked six days a week her entire life as a dental hygienist. If she hadn't, we would not have had a roof over our heads or food on the table, as my stepfather was one of those dreamers who chased the gold at the end of the rainbow. I didn't fully appreciate how hard my mother worked—and how much it cost her—until I was much older. At sixty-three, she looked and felt like seventy-three. Frankly, most women her age did.

When I compare pictures of my mother and me at the same age, I am truly surprised. I thought I would look much older, with more gray hair, more pronounced wrinkles and age spots, and certainly with less energy. I've been told I look ten years younger than I am, and while my memory is not as good as it used to be, most of my faculties seem to be in order.

I have a theory about this—actually two theories. The first is, I have no biological children of my own. I think kids age you immensely. I have a lifelong friend whom I have known since age nine. We are exactly the same age, but she has four kids and looks ten years older. While I did raise my husband's kids, they were nine and eleven at the time they came into my life, so I skipped their infancy period, and instead got their lovely adolescent period. That would age anyone, but I rose above it.

My second theory is that while baby boomers continue to age, there are far more anti-aging products on the market than ever before. My mother would have laughed at an anti-aging product when she was in her sixties. "How could anything be anti-aging?" I can hear her say. Today's baby boomer refuses to look, feel, or act like their parents at the same age.

That's not to say my mother didn't care about her appearance; quite the opposite. Like her mother before her, she was vain; she would have her hair done every week and would get dressed every day of her life, even if she was staying at home all day. She always looked presentable, although smoking for seventy years certainly took its toll on her appearance.

I haven't faced my biggest challenge as yet. I have overcome cancer, heart surgery, and too many maladies to mention. I was my mother's caretaker for the last few years of her life (she died at eighty-eight, my aunt at ninety-eight, my grandmother at ninety-seven, so longevity is in my genes)—but those challenges are nothing compared to what lies ahead, or what so many others have had to endure. Two years ago, I was diagnosed with Parkinson's disease, and I expect that to be a challenge, but I hope to face it with courage, grace, and the good Lord's blessing.

My wants and desires have definitely changed over the last ten years. Ten years ago, I wanted to work for the rest of my life, as long as the quality of my work stood up to time. Now, I just want to get through the next seven years so I can retire, travel, and spend what little time I may have remaining with the love of my life—my husband of thirty-two years, Emil—and my dear friends.

I'm reminded of a line from the movie, "Bridge of Spies." Tom Hanks, who plays a lawyer, says to the spy he is representing, "Aren't you worried—about your family, about the future?" And the spy, Rudolf Abel, says, "Would it help?"

I don't have time to worry about what tomorrow may bring. I hope to live a long, productive life, to enjoy my friends and family for as long as I am able, but beyond that, I have made no future plans. Because I have no biological children of my own, I'm not counting on anyone or any institution to take care of me. I hope by that time there will be a graceful and dignified way for me to exit this life, with little pomp or circumstance.

I am most happy when I am with my husband. We are birds of a feather, best friends who enjoy doing everything together, from grocery shopping, to running errands, to just sitting in front of the TV, watching our favorite shows or movies. This past weekend, Emil came home Friday night at 4:30, and we didn't leave the house until Monday morning. I don't know many couples who can spend an entire weekend, content with one another in one place. Nary a fight, disagreement, or ill word was said. We binge-watched the Netflix series, *Making a Murderer*, and enjoyed it immensely, and talked about it quite a lot.

I know so many women my age, give or take a few years, who are unhappy in their relationships or frustrated with their particular status quo. A former therapist once told me, "There comes a time in every person's life when you will no longer put up with what you've been putting up with." That's not me, and I suspect if you were to ask my husband, he would say the same. We are used to one another, and we don't let the petty disagreements that haunted those first few years of our marriage invade our lives today. We are content and loving. Emil writes me love emails every day, makes me laugh every day, several times a day, and tells me, "I fall in love with you all over again, every day of my life." I feel the same. How blessed are we?

I have fun with my hubby watching TV, and we love to go to the movies. Or we can just sit on the couch, each reading our books, for hours on end. We love to travel and are perfect travel buddies. When one wants to stop and maybe rest a bit, the other one is fine with that. When one is ready to get up and go, so does the other. Hubby and I hope to take a Christmas cruise to Germany this year.

Today, I would say to my eighteen-year-old self, "Don't be afraid of failure." I was so sure if I aimed for the stars, I would fail, and so I didn't take many risks early on in my life. I wish I had. Instead of searching for a secure, safe, nine-to-five job, I wish I had tried harder to reach my ultimate goal—to be Sally Rogers on the old *Dick Van Dyke* show. I wanted to be a staff writer on a sitcom, but the business is paved with failures. Even the very best writers get rejected, and I reached a point where I just couldn't face another redlined script. So I turned to advertising, where I excelled for many years. But there is still that "Sally Rogers" part of me that wishes I had gone for it—come hell or high water.

In Our Seventies

Colors of Life
Kathryn Holmes

L ife is a masterpiece. Like a painting, we start out with a single color and with each experience and challenge we add more colors. We have a choice as to what colors we add and how we portray them.

When I was ten years old, I was heartbroken when the boy I was stalking threw a broom at me. That was a bright color which has now faded and been replaced with more dynamic and vibrant colors.

Each year, we add more color to our palette. Some colors are soft and peaceful, while others are striking and dominant.

The German philosopher Friedrich Nietzsche said, "What does not kill me makes me strong." In 2012, Kelly Clarkson used similar words in her song "Stronger." Scientific studies have shown that small amounts of trauma can make us more resilient.

I was fortunate that I was born into a family of strong women. My grandmother was up feeding and caring for her family shortly after the home delivery of every one of her twelve children. My mother had only an eighth-grade education and worked her way up to becoming an office manager while raising me on her own. Not only were they sturdy, determined women, but had the ability to overcome obstacles in their lives. Each hill I needed to surmount was followed by an even greater one, often turning into a mountain. Although sometimes I felt as if I would be defeated, my fortitude and persistence helped me to overcome each challenge.

During my younger years, heartbreak was my biggest challenge. Later, after my marriage dissolved, I continued to raise my two children on my own, balancing family, work, and a limited budget, with little time to regenerate myself. I was fortunate enough to lose my job.

Fortunate, you say? Shortly after that, I was given the opportunity and funding to start a small business. Beginning at ground zero and working it into a successful business was an experience that gave me the confidence I needed to tackle future career choices. I became publisher of a real estate newspaper and created a women's business and professional magazine. I had ambition, desire, and the tenacity to realize my career dreams. My canvas conveyed bursts of bright orange, neon pink, and brilliant turquoise. Creativity was in full swing.

As my kids were becoming young adults, I began battling health issues. Each one was greater than the last. I almost went into a coma, and it would have been difficult to revive me if I hadn't had my hypothyroidism diagnosed. The doctor first dismissed my symptoms as fatigue, but only through my insistence was I referred to another doctor, who made the diagnosis.

Years later I began to experience extreme fatigue. After numerous visits to a variety of doctors and extensive tests, the doctors still did not know what was wrong. I continued to drag myself to work every day. At the brink of complete exhaustion, I pleaded with my doctors to find out what was wrong with me. I was admitted to the hospital and diagnosed with a pulmonary embolism. Had the blood clots in my lungs traveled to my heart, I would have been dead.

Next was the breast cancer scare. Fortunately, my breast cancer was diagnosed early and was very small. A lumpectomy and radiation treatments have kept me clear for fifteen years. However, the lumpectomy surgery left me with another pulmonary embolism. This time I was put on a blood thinner for the rest of my life.

Again, I challenged the doctors when I came down with a rare autoimmune disease that took months to diagnose. The disease caused my immune system to attack all my healthy cells, especially in my kidneys and lungs. Left unchecked, it would have been fatal. After undergoing a year of chemotherapy and heavy doses of prednisone, the disease went into remission.

Five years later it returned. After months of chemotherapy and prednisone treatment, I began to get weaker instead of stronger. One evening I collapsed in my bedroom doorway and was unable to move from the waist down to my toes. I was diagnosed with a damaged spine which was caused by the fat deposits from the prednisone that had lodged in my already weakened osteoporosis-laden spine. Doctors told me I would be paralyzed for the rest of my life.

My canvas was painted with muddy grays.

As months passed, it turned into a sea of blue with fine streaks of lemon yellow as I tried to do the best I could with what I had. The black and blues represent the fatigue and exhaustive physical therapy I endured. When I could stand for three minutes, and then get from my bed to my wheelchair, my canvas was painted with orange and yellow as a sign of hope. Soon I was walking with a walker and traversing steps.

I never thought I would walk again. Today, my career dreams have dissipated. Not in a sad way, for they left like a cloud in the sky moving on to leave room for a sunny day. My life is more peaceful now. I feel blessed to be able to take my dog for a walk twice a day through the wooded path across from our condo. I can play hide-and-seek with my granddaughters. I have a loving husband and a life that allows me to choose what projects I want to get involved in and still have time to enjoy a good book. Life is good!

The desire to travel and seek adventure in different countries was never realized until after I was forty years old. My husband and I were fortunate enough to travel to places I never dreamed I would ever see. Now my husband is confined to a wheelchair, so we don't travel much. The wandering, flowing colors in my canvas are more stable now. The desire to travel has faded, but not completely disappeared.

I still tackle projects, like when I wrote the book about my journey from paralysis to walking. Also, I submit inspirational articles for books written by others. My marketing background comes in handy when I can help other authors promote themselves or work on special projects for my church. I am pleased I am still productive, although not as agile as I once was.

The voyage of life is filled with rocky roads, but we can still move on, often to a better and more fulfilling existence. As I look back, I realize I should have gone to bed when I was sick instead of pretending the earth would go into a holding pattern if I weren't there for the day. I would never have insisted the car windows be rolled up on a summer day because my hair had just been teased and sprayed.

We have choices in life.

We can choose what colors we paint on our canvas.

The Secrets and Miracles of Life
Janie Jasin

Watching the courage of my godmother and my dad's sister Emma's wisdom and communication was an example of smart goodness pouring out of ninety- and one-hundred-five-year-old women.

The Littlest Christmas Tree is a best seller which was written in duress as I was crying and walking in the Christmas tree fields in Wisconsin. I was an only child and not empowered with power of attorney, which left me in crisis about how to connect with clients while overseeing two parents with Alzheimer's disease, Parkinson's disease, and dementia. I wrote the one-page story; a publisher saw it and it became a miracle.

Earlier, at age thirty-six, my decision to seek sobriety and live a life of twelve steps became a touchstone for a career, family, and a life. I began to live in gratitude and acceptance.

I value my wisdom, experience, and connections in work. I was blessed as an author of a bestselling book, speaking engagements, and talking to groups from ten to two-thousand. That excitement keeps my creativity humming. What was once so vital, however, is now a small part of my life.

I continue to write, coach speaking students and maintain relationships with church, family, and career dynamos. I want to give more away and to use the talent I have.

I live at the lake of my childhood from May to October each year. The pines, the water, and the inspiration are mighty. My other life is in Minnesota, where chums of my speaking world meet and there is family nearby. Many say, "Winter in Minnesota, summer in Wisconsin." Oh well, it turned out that way, and I am blessed.

I have fun with friends who are fun and funny, with a depth of character, brilliance, and creativity. They speak, write, serve, pray, and we laugh as we work at delivering our best selves to each other.

My words of love to you are:

Relax, take risks, and lean on what makes you excited about learning. Serve others, watch them, and ask them questions about their journey. Don't worry about what your parents think you should do. Follow your love, and dream your own dreams. Don't worry about marriage, children, and houses. Jump into your passionate creative self. Find a mentor, read, and learn to laugh at yourself.

The Journey of an Independent Spirit
Karen Lund

Reflecting on my life at seventy-five, it's clear to me that my life was truly guided by the Universe. I never set goals, and I never asked myself or anyone else, "Why am I here?" or "What is my purpose in life?" This reflection says I wasn't very philosophical in thinking about life. I just did what was presented to me. I don't remember questioning, "Should I or should I not?" again, I just *did*.

I've lived a full life, experienced great adventures, and haven't been lonely, even though I lived alone for fifty years. My life is enjoyable. I'm busy, and more importantly, I'm involved in my community and various issues in the world. Actually, I'm just involved in *life*. Happiness is a decision I made.

My career has been my life. It evolved from one set of skills developed in my preparation to become a teacher, to continuously adding skills through a number of careers. I was trained as a teacher at a state teachers college; a very practical approach. I learned planning, scheduling, setting objectives, measuring performance, and the art of teaching, which is interacting with students. I implemented these skills with seventh- and eighth-graders.

After five years of teaching, I moved on to become a recreation director in military hospitals during the Vietnam War. This experience taught me the skills of working with and managing a staff—a staff of volunteers. Ninety percent of the recreation activities were completed by volunteers. Development and training were critical for the staff. When your activity schedule is from 10:00 a.m. to 10:00 p.m., seven days a week, it can only be accomplished with staff who have a great desire to be of service. Through the dedicated volunteer staff, this program was offered during the two years I was stationed at the Navy hospital on Guam.

This led me directly into the business world of consulting. I used all of these skills, but first had to take the language of education and convert it to business language. The skills were the same for these two worlds, nonprofit or for-profit. For more than thirty-five years, my consulting offered me the opportunity to work in about a hundred industries, in companies in the United States as well as Singapore, Malaysia, Hong Kong, Thailand, Australia, New Zealand, and Canada. I just did it because I could.

I had responsibility for development and training of local professional staff. I also worked directly with employees in their work environment and was often in manufacturing facilities. One just happened to be a Barbie doll factory in Malaysia. In Australia, I worked in one of the largest silver, zinc, and copper mines in the world. It was so large we drove around in trucks underground.

My challenges always came from within. Why did I not have more friends? Why didn't I get the promotions that I believed should have been mine? Why wasn't I liked? Not much of my time was spent on these questions. I would think about them and then ignore the issue. I didn't talk to anyone about these concerns, as I didn't think anyone would care. I didn't think about how others could help me, support me, and even mentor me. I just did.

Maybe at eighteen, having a better understanding of just who I was and how my internal struggles could be diminished by asking for help would have been of benefit to me.

I now know this independent spirit gave me the confidence to just do whatever was before me. Often it allowed me to be me. Along with my independent spirit, today I realize the Universe knew I needed these life experiences in order to gain the insight and wisdom for my purpose. I wasn't aware of my purpose. I didn't dream big dreams—maybe not even little dreams.

When I was in my early fifties, I had to venture out on my own, and I say "had to" because I was fired. It was a great decision that others made for me. It introduced to me to development and growth that created new skills and enhanced old ones. I was able to create my own consulting principles for delivering the services of productivity and profitability. Later, I connected with the Core Passion Company, and am now a partner.

Traveling and working as a consultant in other countries enlightened me to the differences and similarities among cultures, governments, traditions, and most importantly, people. At the human level, we all seem to have desires, dreams, and challenges. We want to grow and learn. In order to become a citizen of the world, we need to understand the similarities and differences between us and to accept them.

I believe and feel my purpose is to offer ways others can strive for peace in whatever aspect of life they desire peace. Furthermore, I offer them, through writing, speaking, and conducting workshops, ideas, habits, traditions, and behaviors focused on the courage to act. I just released my first book, *Being an Elder.* An elder is one "who has wisdom and experience and lives their life with humility and gratitude."

Our world continues to offer all of us the opportunity to have a more fulfilling, meaningful, and joyful life. When kindness, hope, compassion, and love are our behaviors, we are strong citizens of the world. My life always has been and always will be about adventures, fun, growth, learning, and challenges. I will continue to do whatever the Universe decides is important for me, in whatever is offered.

Life Is What You Make It
Gloria VanDemmeltraadt

I don't believe that anyone is truly "prepared" for life. Each one of us is a product of our environment and experiences, coupled with our individual personalities. A number of bad things happened along my path in life, and I endured some tough times. However, my faith in God and the amazing strength He provided have helped me to use the bad times to strengthen myself even more.

As the years passed, I have looked at each phase as the best, and to my continued wonderment, they keep getting better. Each phase presents its challenges, of course, but appreciation for my intellect, my healthy body, my ability to love, and my gratitude and joy in being grows greater and greater with each passing year.

I married at age eighteen, and after seven years, while I was pregnant with my third child, my husband left us and ran off to California with a young girl. I went through a period of more than four years alone, having to support three babies with no education and little money.

I worked in an office during the day and served drinks and sang in a bar at night. I lived with my college student brother for a time and hoped to go to college myself. There was no money, however, and extra hours at my night job were needed to merely survive. How we made it through this terrible time I have to say was by the grace of God. There were times of hunger and doubt, and many sleepless nights filled with fear.

Three tiny children made me a big package of baggage in trying to find a husband who might be willing to take me on. I kept looking because I saw no other option. Eventually, I married a brave widower with two teenagers. My husband traveled, which made life difficult, but we combined our families, had one more child, and raced through the years building a life for all of us. I never went hungry again, but there were more bad times when my husband's business collapsed and we lost our house and all of our savings. We rebuilt our lives with perseverance, resolve, and lots of laughter.

My wants and desires have changed significantly over the last decade. In addition to the illness and death of my husband, I developed severe hearing loss, which terminated my singing vocation. I learned that when a door closes, God opens a window. Not only did I meet and marry another kind and caring man, I began writing and have embarked on an incredibly rewarding writing and speaking career.

My plans for the future are to write, read, and repeat. My husband and I cherish each day we have together, and we support each other in the myriad activities in which we are involved. My speaking events are increasing because of my three published books, and I do all I can to help new writers get started. I also encourage people to capture their memories in written form. The past is the root in all of us, and it is important for future generations to know their heritage in order to build on it. I will continue to write life stories for hospice patients and others, and am now taking classes on learning to write fiction. This might be my next new career.

I am blessed with good health and am determined to do all I can to stay healthy. I am extremely involved in volunteer work, which I find rewarding. My six children are on their own, with families and active lives. Letting them go gives me great relief. I recognize I no longer have control over their decisions, and this is wonderfully freeing. All I can do from this point on is to love them and let them know I love them.

Relationships are the most important thing in life, and I would qualify that to say *good relationships*. I no longer waste time on bad-tempered or grouchy people. I keep myself surrounded by fun people who enjoy life as I do. I am blessed to have a great husband with a delightful sense of humor and we both believe that a day without laughter is a day wasted. Life is what you make it, and we make it fun just being together. Onno, my husband, and I eat out often, spend time with family and good friends, and travel as much as we can.

Playing cards with a great group of friends is wonderful fun, and we laugh the whole day while trying to solve the world's problems. Wine helps, too.

There's a saying that goes, "We become too soon old, and too late smart." How true at any age! When I turned eighteen, I was intensely involved in planning my wedding to my high-school sweetheart in less than a month's time. This marriage was a foolish and desperate attempt to do what I thought was expected of me. Sadly, I didn't reach out, nor did I have others in my life to guide me in making better decisions about what to do with my life after high school. I was afraid and insecure and latched onto what seemed at the time to be my only option.

My advice for young people today would be to talk freely and frankly with others before making major life decisions. Similar-age friends are okay, but parents are better. If they are not available, look to school guidance counselors; pastors; 4-H, scouting, and other youth group leaders; and don't forget parents of friends. Make lists of options and above all, listen to your own heart.

Think long and hard about what you want to get out of life before taking major steps. Guidance is important, from above and from those we respect. But in the end, life is truly what you make it.

In Our Eighties

You Are Never Too Old to Stop Learning
Marnie Hensel

Until a few years ago, I was a downhill ski racer. As a result of this sport, I have had sixty-four orthopedic surgeries. The hardest part of any surgery is the rehabilitation to get your body back into decent shape. Having had to do this since I was twenty-one has given me the experience to have patience and work hard to achieve my desires.

I have always had a strong faith and have believed that I was given these experiences so I could help others who might be going through the same things. I also took a course at the University of Minnesota in health coaching so I could help my friends who wanted someone to give them advice and go with them to medical appointments.

As a result of all those surgeries, I spent a lot of time in hospitals and even more time in gyms getting my body what I considered back to normal. When you are in your twenties, it is not a lot of fun to be on crutches all the time. I always wanted to continue skiing and racing, so I had a goal to return to top physical and mental shape.

In this particular area of my life, I was amply rewarded for the work I had put into keeping in shape. At age seventy-three, I won a national medal in giant slalom in Park City, Utah. Achieving that goal reinforced my efforts to always stay as healthy as I could.

Some wants and desires have changed, and some have not. Once I received the national gold medal, I no longer made ski racing such a prominent part of my life. From the time I was first injured, I have been a motivational speaker, trying to help people adjust their attitude so they can more easily achieve their desires. I still very much enjoy continuing that practice.

My goals over the last ten years have been to remain healthy so I can continue to travel, to maintain the special relationships I have nurtured with my large family and wonderful friends, and to make new friends along the way—especially younger ones.

Just recently, my youngest granddaughter graduated from high school. I have thirteen grandchildren and almost seven great-grandchildren. When my grands turned thirteen years old, I took each one of them alone with me on a trip to a destination of their choice. As a result of those special trips, I have a very close relationship with those children. One of my future plans is to try to get to know the great-grandchildren even better than I do now. They might be a bit young now to travel great distances, but there are other ways to get to know them.

Eleven years ago, the Mayo Clinic discovered I had stage 1 lung cancer. Surgery removed part of my lung, and the cancer has never returned.

I've always done volunteer work for places like the Center for Spirituality and Healing in Minneapolis, but I am now looking forward to being a volunteer for the one-year-old Gilda's Club in Minnetonka. It is my way of giving back for a happy result of my own cancer.

I was fortunate to have a very special husband for forty-four years. Carl died eleven years ago, and a day doesn't go by that I don't miss him. Three years ago I met another very special man, and we have been close friends ever since. I really love my lady friends, but it is awfully nice to have a gentleman friend as well.

Most of my very large family lives within fifteen minutes of me. One granddaughter and her husband and their little girl live in Indianapolis, but they return to Minnesota quite often.

I really love my townhouse right on a beautiful lake and within very easy driving distance of downtown Minneapolis. I still go to a fitness center six days a week, so my health is excellent for my age. I also continue to teach water aerobics at a friend's pool in the summer. I taught pool and studio aerobics at my fitness center for twenty-five years and retired five years ago.

I try to have fun every day. As well as working on keeping my body in good shape, I try to work on my brain as well. I've played bridge since college days, but had stopped when Carl died. Playing the hands has not really changed all that much since then, but the bidding is like an entirely new game. Six months ago, I started taking lessons so I could learn about the different way to bid, and I now play bridge twice a week and love every minute of it. Another way I have fun is to take courses. There are so very many wonderful colleges in the Twin Cities, and most of them offer courses to seniors for the small sum of ten dollars. Just going to classes on those campuses makes me feel young.

I enjoy writing. My paternal grandmother and maternal great-grandmother both have written their memoirs. I decided I should write mine, and I have. Going over your life like that is something I felt was a great deal of fun. I also enjoyed the feeling of contributing to our family history.

Several years ago, I learned how to play drums and I now am a member of the Smith College drum team.

Last, but not least, I have fun going to the movies. Every Friday I read the reviews of the newest films and pick one film I want to see.

The one piece of advice that I would give myself is to *listen*. Not only to advice other people give me, but to really listen to my own intuition. I was a people-pleaser, and there were times I did what I thought my parents or my teachers or my friends thought I should do. This was not always what I felt deep down was the right thing to do. The older I get, the more attention I pay to what I think I should do in spite of what others might want me to do.

You're Never Too Old to Enjoy Life
Gisela Lee

In preparation for this period of my life, I have to look back on my mother's advice. She taught me to take any pain that comes and make the best of it. She said, "Don't look at the negative; always look for the good and make the best of it." She had had many bad experiences during World War II, and she learned to always look for the positive; she taught me to do that, too.

The greatest challenge I've overcome in my life was moving to the United States. I left my comfortable and established home and family in Germany at the age of twenty-one and immigrated to the United States. At that point, I hadn't seen the man who was to be my husband for eighteen months, and I felt like I really didn't know him. I didn't know anyone else in the U.S., either, and the differences in culture, language, and absolutely everything were huge and terrifying.

When I was very young, I would go on long bike trips with my girlfriend. We'd be gone for as long as two weeks, and we had no money. We stayed in youth hostels and had stimulating exploits with strangers along the way. We had no fear—no anxiety about potential dangers—we were curious and eager for adventure.

I had been in college in Munich, Germany, in 1954, when I met Jack Lee, an American soldier, from Minnesota. Jack was an acquaintance of my roommate, who had served as a chaperone for her to go to parties because German girls weren't allowed to go out alone. Later on, my friend invited Jack for a drink to thank him for chaperoning her, and I was also invited. Even though I was Catholic and he was Protestant, I was German and he was an American, and he was a soldier—a big no-no for a good German girl—I was fascinated with him. And he with me, as well. I was seriously warned to not get involved with a soldier, but I ignored this advice. I was adventuresome and excited by life, and we fell in love.

Jack went back to Minnesota and we continued to write and call each other. Eventually, he said if I wouldn't come to the U.S., he would go to Germany and try to find work there. After many difficulties and warnings by my family, I decided to go to Jack.

Following a long and terrible series of flights and bus rides (including having a seatmate vomit all over me), having nothing but five marks to my name (just over a dollar), and very little to eat, I was finally reunited with tall and handsome Jack, who, after eighteen months of separation, seemed like a complete stranger to me.

My story is too long to tell here, but we were eventually married. We still are, and we have had a wonderful life. All this, in spite of a rocky and scary beginning for me, with poor English, no friends, and serious culture shock.

My wants and desires have significantly changed over the past ten years. I sold my long-term decorating business, and my husband and I sold our big house and moved in to a townhouse that's easier to take care of. Now we are in the process of selling our precious cabin in Wisconsin, where we spent many years with joyous family-and-friend gatherings. We are just not able to do the work anymore, and we decided it's time for someone else to enjoy the cabin.

In the future, I want to travel more for fun now that my business obligations are finished. I do a lot of volunteer work, for the church particularly, but I'm even cutting back on those responsibilities. Enjoying life is a priority now more than ever. My family makes me happy. I have two great children who love me, and wonderful grandchildren. I still have family in Germany and I talk with them often. I also have lots of good friends, and we have fun together. My plans for the future get simpler all the time. Right now, being alive and staying healthy and happy are my goals.

Fun is a bigger part of my life as I get older. I play cards with a great group of women and we laugh all the time. We go out to eat now and then, and that's great fun. I have another good group of friends with whom I have coffee every week. I like to exercise to stay in shape. Staying busy is important to me; there is always something to do. I've noticed as I get older that I focus on the things I enjoy rather than the things that have to be done.

If I could go back to give my eighteen-year-old self advice, I have to say, in spite of things turning out well in the end, I should not have fallen in love with a foreigner. I have no regrets for marrying Jack, but if I hadn't known him, I would most likely have married someone in my native country. I believe I should have stayed in Germany as a young girl. Young people have no fear. Life is exciting and it's easy to get taken over by thrilling new adventures.

As we get older, we become more cautious, and I have times when I really miss my homeland and the family I left behind in Germany. When I left for America with stars in my eyes, I didn't realize what a huge change it would be. My advice would be to think long and hard before taking such a drastic step.

My Attitude and Gratitude
Renee Soskin

How does one begin to write only a few paragraphs about a life that has been so blessed with wonderful experiences—yet had so many heartbreaking chapters to overcome?

I grew up in a small town in South Dakota and loved every moment of it. My friends and classmates were a big part of my life. My parents were giving and intellectually stimulating, and they helped me to be responsible and mature. Their business, having general stores, gave me a great education. School was fun in junior and senior high, and I was a cheerleader and queen. After school, I was a window dresser and washer, a salesperson, sign painter, and bookkeeper. For my school and county, I was selected as a DAR (Daughters of the American Revolution) candidate.

I went to the University of Minnesota, where I met my wonderful husband, Sid, who was also a student and teacher. I was very active on campus. Sid and I dated, married, and went to Europe, where he studied and worked in hospitals in Zurich, London, and Vienna. It was a most exciting long honeymoon.

On returning home, my husband worked at Mount Sinai hospital in Cleveland, Ohio, in orthopedic residency. I then became president of the Women's Medical Auxiliary. I was always so lucky to have these unexpected positions, and always learned from them.

We had three sons and moved to Des Moines, Iowa, for his career as an orthopedic surgeon. It was a very special community to me, and I loved it. I was president of the Park County Medical Auxiliary. We raised money for a new science center. I was also vice president of sisterhood and on the board of trustees of our synagogue. I then decided to start a business, because I could never say "no" to the many leadership roles offered to me. I became a convention planner and did anything needed to help with tours, spouse programs, or entertainment. My husband was very proud and supportive of all my endeavors.

At fifty years old, my husband passed away playing tennis. Our youngest son was developmentally disabled, and friends and I started a special school staffed with many volunteers to enrich the lives of children like him. I also helped start a group home for adults; we were the last such home funded by HUD in the United States. I never thought it would play such a part in my future, as my son Bennett was the very youngest at the time.

My business was thriving thanks to a lot of free publicity. My two other sons were doing well, too. One was at Washington University and one was at MIT, and a few years later at Boston University Law School.

My husband's family introduced me to a wonderful man from Minneapolis. We fell in love, and thus began another chapter in my life. I moved to Minneapolis and my son chose to stay in Des Moines, as he felt he had helped build the house that we had started. As a child he cut the ribbon and broke the ground—so that was his.

I have had many opportunities offered to me, and I felt lucky even if I had to say "no" to some of them. It was amazing to know how many chances there are out there and available to women. In many ways I felt like a pioneer.

My husband, Arnie, passed away after a long battle with cancer, but we had a good quality of life between surgical and treatment episodes. We were able to enjoy many things. He, as well as Sid, my first husband, came with me to my reunions in South Dakota, to see my roots.

I also had the misfortune of being involved in a fraudulent stock market deal. Not only did I lose my loved ones, but also my money as well. But life goes on, in spite of all the twists and turns. I remain ever grateful and happy for my experiences. I am a lucky person, and I've learned a lot during my years. I still am very active, with sports, reading, movies, theater, and travel.

There is no truth to the saying, "it's a man's world." We, as women, are too big a part of it. I do think luck, intuition, and perseverance help us through our events.

I was especially pleased and lucky to go to China with Governor Robert Ray of Iowa, to set up Friendship Force there, and it helped me more appreciate what we have in our country.

My lifelong philosophy has been, "One door closes and another one opens." We just have to be courageous.

My desires are to find fulfillment in all my activities. I find most days are filled with fun whether with friends or books.

You have to take life as it comes, and make the right choices. And face life with a positive attitude.

Proud to Be a Woman!
Bev Tangan

I'm eighty-five years old, speeding toward eighty-six with my foot tapping to the beat of my personal theme song, "I Am Woman," by Helen Reddy. The song, based on her life experiences, became the theme song for the United Nations International Woman's Year in 1975, and her words still ring true today.

How I loved that song. It symbolized the way I felt about myself, about being a woman, and life as it was in the seventies. During the fifties, I had a job I loved. In the mid-sixties, my job turned into a career, but it was the next decade that challenged me to survive in a so-called man's field. In spite of my dad's warning—"They won't let you in, and I don't want you to get hurt"—I was determined to succeed, even if it did hurt.

My journey started in the middle of the Second World War. Women rushed to fill the jobs left open as men joined the armed services. The country was united in patriotic involvement with the war effort. My father, a display manager for a specialty shop, repeatedly turned down my offer to fill in for his missing crew. Finally, he gave up, and having gained permission from the state, he agreed to hire me part-time as long as I signed a contract. Thirteen years old, and I had my second contract (the first at age eleven, when I signed my life away in order to get my hair cut). This time the contract was stiffer: not only did I have to follow the rules, but I had to fork over some of my paycheck to war bonds. This was a small price to pay in order to begin my career destiny. I was going to be a displayer, even though my dad repeatedly told me, "it's a man's job," and my mom told me to "be a teacher; it's more ladylike."

However, at age thirteen, my goal was clear: I was going to help win the war, and then aim for the top job: window trimmer.

The war ended, soldiers returned, the economy surged, suburbs became the new frontier, and a lot of women remained in the work world. Our feminist-sisterhood had begun.

The war bonds became savings bonds after the war ended and paid for college. After I graduated, I moved to the big city and joined a department store, where I continued dressing mannequins and climbing ladders. Every once in a while, the men would let me work in the display windows.

The sixties were fun. I stopped working for a few years to care for my twin boys. During the mid-sixties, I returned to the display world, where the joy of painting with merchandise and finding the perfect fashion for my beloved mannequins filled my days.

It was the seventies that opened opportunities for women. It was an inspirational decade of sisterhood; women tossed away the bra and the apron (unless they wore it under a chef's hat). After the emancipation of skirt lengths in the sixties, we were pants-wearing feminists looking for equality with our brothers in the work world. We read self-help books, confidently dared to attend events alone, and learned to expect and ask for promotions or raises. We were interested in meditation, yoga, self-improvement, eating well, and planning our next goal. Above all, we were positive thinkers.

One night, I placed so many self-help books on the counter at the bookstore, I was asked if I had a problem. And one day when I was between jobs, my son said, "You know, mom, we wouldn't be in such a mess if you weren't such a positive thinker."

It was expectations of several enlightened bosses that forced me to step out of my comfort zone and to reach beyond my experience. Their expectations were scary motivators. I found my deepest fulfillment came when challenges that required edgy thinking and outside-the-box solutions actually worked. These challenges were given like gifts with a deadline. My remarkable mentors gave me something priceless when they pushed me to do that which sounded impossible, something beyond anything I had previously done. In an effort not to disappoint, I often ended up surprising myself.

Today, women are no longer relegated to the mannequin room, or the register; they can now move into the top job. A lot of passion and drive made this happen, and it began during the war. It continued through the following decades of female empowerment and dedication.

I now live in a beautiful, brand new apartment with a balcony overlooking the Los Angeles Railroad Yards and the distant San Gabriel Mountains. It's a mixed-use complex in the Arts District neighborhood of Los Angeles. My building looks like a train and feels like a ship. The retail stores are a wonderful source of fascination as I watch their progress, slowly working toward their future grand openings. It's like vicariously reliving parts of my past as I walk around this ever-expanding community. I call myself a retail street critic who walks a dog.

Retirement has been a tremendous and glorious surprise. Once I went to a company management meeting where a retirement fund was presented. I whispered to an associate, "I don't plan to retire. Whatever would I do? I love to work." I remember he responded, "I can't wait." I thought he was nuts.

I place a great deal of importance on loving what you do. Both of my sons grew up knowing I worked to put food on the table, but loved going to work every day. It gives me great joy to see them follow that path. Their passions feed my soul as I watch them experience the love of solving problems with creative solutions and professional integrity.

The display industry was a man's domain, but through hard work, talent, and determination, that is no longer true. Women have become a creative force, adding imagination and flair to the display world that now calls itself "visual merchandising." It makes me proud to have been a part of history.

The advice I would give to anyone, including my eighteen-year-old self: Appreciate praise. Value constructive criticism. Expect negative feedback. Listen to all three, but don't allow it to become personal. It's a waste of time and emotion to feel insecure. Instead, choose to focus on your strengths, and look for opportunities to expand them.

In Our Nineties

Listen and Accept
Geanne Jepsen

From the time I was in high school, I planned to be a nurse, or thought I might work in an orphanage or someplace like that. I had a deep need to take care of people. As it turned out, I took care of people in other ways—God had another plan for me. I had three daughters, one of them adopted, and my husband was ill for a long time, so I took care of him. We also became lifetime foster parents to a mentally challenged baby boy.

Another related event was that my father's mother was an invalid for most of her life. On the day I was married and moved out of my parents' home, my grandmother moved in. I watched my mother take care of her mother-in-law for most of the rest of her life.

The reason I believe these experiences prepared me for this stage of my life, is that upon recently having reached the age of ninety-two, I have learned that even though I have been a care-taker for most of my life, I don't want to be taken care of. I cherish my independence. And I want to hold onto it as tightly as possible for as long as possible.

The greatest challenge I've had in my life is bringing up my foster boy. We were told at the outset what the trials might be involved in taking on a child with brain damage, and we were warned about the vast need of patience and perseverance. As the years went by and we loved him more and more, the future became scarier as we realized the weight of this lifetime commitment.

My wants and desires have changed significantly over the past ten years. My husband, Art, passed away seven years ago after a long period of illness and memory failure. I never dreamed that my husband could have something like that happen to him, and it was all very hard to accept. I had never lived alone until that time, and it has been an adjustment. However, I've learned that life can still be good without Art, and without all of my family at home. My daughters have families of their own, and my son, while he will never be completely independent, lives in a building for people with special needs.

I've learned to appreciate my quiet times, and I've certainly kept myself busy with many activities. I've learned to appreciate my home, and I like being able to come and go as I please. I am content to be on my own.

My future plans are to remain in my home and continue being a hospice volunteer for as long and as often as patients need me. When the time comes when I might need help myself, I would rather have someone come in to help instead of moving to a nursing facility.

I am happy that I am able to live on my own, that I can still drive where I want to go, and that I can be involved and active in life. Keeping my intellect is a huge blessing, which I appreciate greatly after watching my husband suffer the loss of memory and the indignities that happen as a result of that sad affliction.

I have fun just living. I've always been a glass-half-full type of person, and laughter is an important part of my life. I have a wonderful loving family and many dear friends. I'm involved in fun things, like a singing group that meets weekly, and I'm thrilled that I can still reach the high notes. There's a group called Caring Connections for widows and widowers which meets for dinner monthly, and I do calling for them, as well as being part of the group. Another fun thing for me is sitting in a corner and reading a good book. I can travel the world and not have to leave home.

Thinking back to when I was eighteen, I don't know that any advice I could have given myself would have worked. I tried to go on to nursing school, which my mother sincerely wanted me to do. However, not one but two serious and unusual illnesses put a stop to my schooling, and I went home. To my father's delight—and mine—I married the man I had loved since I was in fourth grade. We went on to have sixty-six years of caring and laughter together.

What I realized then, and still appreciate after all these years, was that God had a different plan for me. I just needed to listen to what that plan was—and accept it.

The Nifty Nineties
Muriel Johnson

When I was twenty years old, my mother had a serious stroke. Doctors discovered she had diabetes also, and she spent a month in the hospital. When she came home, I quit my job in a drugstore in Wayzata, Minnesota, and took care of her. I was the youngest in the family, and my seven siblings all had families to care for, so it became my responsibility. Patience has never been my greatest virtue, and I think caring for Mother helped me develop patience.

My father had ulcers, so he wasn't very well himself. They lived on a farm and there were cows to milk, chickens to feed, and many other chores to do.

I had to pump water outside and haul it into the house and heat it on the wood stove. There was a washing machine on the porch and I washed the clothes there with water I had heated on the wood stove. Everyday chores took longer to do back then, because we didn't have the conveniences we take for granted today.

This hard work has served me well throughout my life and now that my husband and I are both in our nineties, I am caring for him, because he is not as fit as I am.

My lack of patience was a problem in my life. Taking care of my mother helped, but raising five children taught me more about being patient. Challenges are part of life, and no life is without them, but patience and persistence help to conquer the greatest challenge.

Physical changes that came with age have forced me to give up doing some things I've always enjoyed, like driving and gardening. Life changes, and we have to adjust to it as we go. My husband and I moved into a small condominium that is easier for us to maintain. I'm adjusting to living in a much smaller space.

We lived on a seventy-acre farm for many years and raised sheep. My husband, John, had a well-drilling business and I was able to quit my job and stay home and work with the sheep. I had someone shear the sheep, but I spun the wool on my spinning wheel and plied it, which is spinning two threads together. I dyed much of my wool using acid dyes, but I like to experiment. One time I used copper pennies and ammonia as a dye, and the wool became a gorgeous green color. I plied it with some merino wool and knitted a beautiful sweater.

Using a large loom, I wove blankets and throws, plus bolts of lovely wool that I used to make coats and capes and shawls and other garments. I also knitted with the yarn, and I still like knitting sweaters and things for my family using yarn that I've also spun.

John and I also worked with stained glass. I would choose the colors and he cut the glass and built lampshades, window hangings, and beautiful pieces of art. Our smaller space doesn't allow for making stained glass anymore.

My plans for the future are to stay as healthy as I can so I can watch my grandchildren and great-grandchildren grow up. I still love to spin and knit, and I also paint. I use smaller canvases now, but I enjoy painting landscapes, and many of my paintings are hanging in our home as well as in the halls of our condominium building. One of my grandchildren wanted a picture of poppies, so I just finished doing a painting for her from a photo I had taken.

My life is comfortable now. I don't have to haul water or take care of sheep, and my family is grown. My children are all on their own, and I am happy they have become nice people. That is gratifying.

I love to make cookies for my grandchildren and to see the smiles on their faces. I like to cook and still find it fun. John and I sit at the kitchen table and just chat. We're still enjoying life together after sixty-eight years of marriage.

If I were eighteen again, I would definitely tell myself to go to college. Education offers more opportunities in life and I can't emphasize enough how important it is.

A Few of Life's Questions
Helen Pattie

I believe the most important thing—or person—that continues to guide and prepare me for this period of life is God's leading, whether I was aware of it or not.

There have been many challenges along life's journey, but as I think of them, the greatest has to be the first: leaving the comfort, security, and love of home to go to Washington, DC, to work at the age of nineteen. I had taken and passed a Civil Service test and was offered work for what was then the War Department in the Surgeon General's Office. I had never been away from home, I knew no one there, and yet a new life was about to begin.

With only the name and address of a hotel which had been given to my brother by a friend who had visited DC years before, my mother and brother drove me there on a Saturday in May, 1941. After driving around the circles of DC, we arrived at the Dixie Hotel on 12th Street. My brother went in to meet the owner to ask if he knew of a place where I could stay. We were invited to his home for dinner the next day. After dinner and a nice visit, I was invited to remain and live with his family. On my first day at work, I was terrified and bewildered, but excited, too. I was thrilled to be in the nation's capital, and while I didn't realize it at first, a new family and friends were to be my future.

There have been a number of changes in my life over the past ten years. One is a change in location having sold my home in Maryland in 2000. I then came to Minnesota nine years ago. It was both a challenge and an opportunity to make new friends and learn to enjoy different experiences. I moved in with my son and daughter-in-law's young family and have an apartment on the lower level of their home. This gives me the freedom to travel without the concern and care of a house.

The gradual loss of hearing and sight continue to make me appreciative of each day. Also, I am not as mobile as I was ten years ago. I don't drive at night or in inclement weather, and I don't take long walks, but enjoy what I can do.

My future plans are as always to enjoy and appreciate each day—travel to visit my children and grandchildren in Massachusetts, London, Paris, Portugal, and more.

I am happy with right now. I am with my loving family and able to travel, read, knit, do crosswords, and enjoy time with friends both near and far. Life continues to be an adventure.

Fun? It depends on how you identify it. My twelve-year-old grandson comes downstairs to visit and throw the ball around. Sometimes we throw it to each other (my exercise for the day) or we will play a game like Farkle or Phase 10. I enjoy a good joke with my older grandson, and he also helps to keep me somewhat computer literate. Getting a call from an old friend makes me smile. I remember times when fun was something more active, while now listening to music or seeing a comedy on TV is enough.

If I could go back and give my eighteen-year-old self advice, it would be, "Don't be afraid!"

Just When I Thought I Had All My Ducks in a Row
Joan Kennedy

As long as I can remember, my life has been laced with abrupt beginnings and endings. In 1927, when I was five years old, our family moved from a small farming community in Sheboygan, Wisconsin, to Minneapolis, Minnesota. My father had a small farm, and he also worked for a textile mill. When the company moved to Minnesota, they brought our family with them.

After several years, the company moved to St. Paul's West Side. At the time, this area was a poor section of St. Paul. It didn't matter to my dad, because he could walk to work. The move affected my mother the most. After three moves away from friends, and having to leave one lovely neighborhood, my mother had a nervous breakdown.

Aunt Mary came to live with us for a short time. Before she returned home to Villard, Minnesota, she and my dad made arrangements for us four children—my brother, Eddy, and my sisters, Dolly, Babe, and me—to go to an orphanage until things at home had changed, and my mother was back with us. Mother was hospitalized, and once released, went to live with a friend because she was not able to care for us. She finally divorced my dad and moved into a small apartment.

I don't remember the day or the month we were taken to St. Joseph's Orphanage. I was ten years old at the time. All I remember is my dad had trouble finding the place. When we finally arrived, it was after dark. The orphanage was a large, five-story, red stone building with huge concrete steps. My dad drove on the circular driveway, and then the four of us followed our dad up the steps to a large, imposing front door. When he rang the doorbell, a nun came to the door and let us in. After we said goodbye to him, our dad walked away. I don't remember if I was sad, or frightened, or both.

The next morning as I woke up in a dormitory full of girls, I realized it was now time for me to get used to a whole new way of life. Little did I know then, my stay there would last for the next five years. The first day started with morning Mass. All the girls wore black veils and sat on one side of the chapel. The boys sat on the opposite side. The nuns sat in the back pews. The girls and boys were segregated in the building, sleeping on different floors, or playing in separate playground areas, and even eating at different ends of the dining hall. I rarely had an opportunity to talk to my brother, with the exception of visiting hours with our parents. It was difficult for us kids during visiting hours, because both of our parents came, and because they were not speaking to each other.

Our parents were allowed to visit us twice a month on Sundays, and this was the only time we were together. The other Sundays were the loneliest days.

Two years later, when I was twelve, I not only worked in the kitchen, I was also old enough to work in the laundry, located in a separate building. It had huge laundry tubs, drying racks, ironing boards, and a large black coal stove in the middle of the room with ledges around it to heat the irons. We'd take the irons off the stove with hot-pads. When the irons cooled down, we put them back on the stove and took another hot iron, and continued ironing. As I recall, there were a lot of scorched clothes and burned knuckles. Strange as it may seem, I enjoyed the years I spent at the orphanage, because in truth, I felt safe.

When I was fifteen, my brother Eddy and I graduated from eighth grade, which meant we could leave the orphanage. My mother was still living away from home. Because there would only be my dad and my brother in the house, I was placed in a foster home, where I stayed for about eight months. Then our dad married a woman named Lena, and we all moved back home. It felt good to be in close contact again with my brother and sisters. We were never all together again.

As I look back to the night when my father walked away and those massive doors at the orphanage closed behind us, I did not cry. I believe I was able to dig down deep inside myself and find the courage to deal with what was happening. That courage has served me well through the years, to deal with all the unexpected twists and turns of my life's journey.

When I think over my life, the biggest challenge I endured was in the winter of 1988. I was sixty-five years old at the time. I had a house fire. The fire not only destroyed my home, it destroyed a speaking business of fifteen years. I lost close to five hundred copies of my first book. I lost all my speaking and promotional material and all my files. I did not have a computer, but I did have a large Rolodex, with all the names, addresses and phone numbers of my clients and business contacts. That too, was destroyed. Overnight, I was out of business.

Before the fire, I had never thought about my age. I was busy working, confident, and goal-oriented. After the fire, I felt old, tired, and emotionally spent.

I moved into an apartment with rented furniture and no personal possessions around me—not even my purse. That too, had been destroyed.

As time went on, I decided to start reading books on aging. I wanted to find out if there was anything positive about this time in my life.

In 1988, the baby boomers had not turned fifty, so there was very little written about aging. One day, I picked up a magazine published by AARP (at that time, officially named the American Association of Retired People). One of the articles said, "The fastest growing age group in this country is people in their eighties." I thought, "Eighties? Well, hot damn, I'm only sixty-five!" At that moment, I knew in my heart I could start over again. I had time to put the pieces together. I went from feeling old and tired to feeling younger, energetic, and motivated. What a great feeling!

I have thought about my wants and desires at this time in my life. I find they haven't changed much over the years. My first desire is to have good health, to feel safe, and then financial security. Staying close to my family and friends is important to me. And finally, I want just to enjoy and be grateful for my life.

My future plans are to stay involved in my speaking profession, to set new goals and have dreams for my future.

I have fun getting together for happy hour with my family or friends with a lot of talking and laughing. I love eating dinner by candlelight, even when I'm alone.

My advice to my eighteen-year-old self would be: Don't look to other people to make your life more than it is. Know deep in your heart that you have the power to create your own life, through your thoughts, words, and desires. Just be very clear about what it is you desire. Finally, on our life's path, we can become strong in all the broken places of the heart.

About the Author

Joan Kennedy is a well-known speaker and author. She was a stay-at-home mom for eighteen years, and at age forty-five, she went back to work as a fashion coordinator for a large department store. At fifty, she became a motivational speaker.

For two years, she presented daily motivational and inspirational messages on an East Coast radio station.

Joan published her first book at age fifty-six; *I Don't Want Much From Life, I Want More.* At eighty-three, she published *What's Age Got to Do with It?* She compiled stories from forty women for the book, *Unlocking the Secrets of Successful Women,* which became an Amazon Best Seller.

Her true passion is helping women to become more confident and empowered. Her message to them is, "You only have one life to live; don't waste it thinking you don't have what it takes."

Joan has spread her philosophy through books and speaking engagements. She has worked with corporations, health care organizations, conventions, conferences, and women of all ages.

At ninety-four, Joan bills herself as the "oldest motivational speaker in the country."

Are you a woman of a certain age?

If you would like to share your story and be considered for a future edition, please send your 1,000 word, edited story to: Mark@IndieBooksIntl.com

Due to the overwhelming response of our first edition, not all stories submitted were accepted.

Thank you!

Contact Information

In Our 20s

Nikki Abramson – nikki@nikkiabramson.com
Anna Bosak – aebosak@gmail.com
Hannah Neuman – hneuman0@gmail.com
Maddy Sevilla – jvdemm@comcast.net

In Our 30s

Kristen Brown – Kristen@happyhoureffect.com
C.E. Sawyer – crystallabathe@gmail.com
Artica Tyner – Dr.ArticaTyner@gmail.com
Meg Wrobel – meghume@gmail.com

In Our 40s

Neda Kellogg – successfullyconnected@gmail.com
Cindy Koebele – Cindy@title-smart.com
Faith McGown – faithmcgown@gmail.com
Renee Usem – reneeusem@me.com

In Our 50s

Amy Kennedy Fosseen – amyfosseen@yahoo.com
Ann LeBlanc – ann.m.leblanc@icloud.com
Georgine Madden – georginemadden@comcast.net
Ellie Peterson – ellie@powerpositiveworkouts.com

In Our 60s

Barb Greenberg – barb@rediscoveringu.com
Louise Griffith – louise@oneshininglight.com
Judith Milton – judi.milton@gmail.com
Colleen Szot – colleen@wonderfulwriter.com

In Our 70s

Kathryn Holmes – k.m.holmes@comcast.net

Janie Jasin – Janie@janiespeaks.com

Karen Lund – karen@BeingAnElder.com

Gloria Van Demmeltraadt – gloriavandem@gmail.com

In Our 80's

Marnie Hensel – marn@attitudeaging.com

Giesel Lee – Gieselee@hotmail.com

Renee Soskin – reneesoskin@yahoo.co

Bev Tangen – bevtang@yahoo.com

In Our 90s

Geanne Jepsen – no contact information available

Muriel Johnson – 440036th Avenue North, #212,
Robbinsdale, MN 55422

Helen Pattie – hppattie@comcast.net

Joan Kennedy – joan@joankennedy.com

Made in the USA
Las Vegas, NV
04 January 2024

83922062R00104